THE DISABLED STUDENT IN HIGHER EDUCATION: ACCESS AND SUPPORT

Report of a conference for the International Year of Disabled People

Edited by

RICHARD HOLMES and FRANCIS APRAHAMIAN

THE OPEN UNIVERSITY PRESS

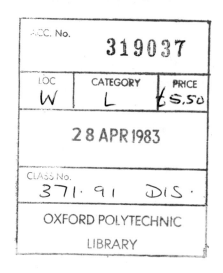
The Open University Press
Walton Hall, Milton Keynes
MK7 6AA

First published 1981

ISBN 0 335 101054

Printed in Great Britain
by the Open University

Contents

Opening address

N.J.D. SMITH

Accom + Mobility

(Chairman of the Advisory Council on the Disabled, Open University)

In opening the day's proceedings, Professor Smith welcomed the participants to the Open University, commenting that it was gratifying to see so many representatives of institutions of higher education from all over Great Britain, and all with an interest or involvement in the education of the disabled. He extended a special welcome to Lord Snowdon, who was participating as the President, for England, of the International Year, and to Dr Rhodes Boyson, the Minister with Responsibility for Higher Education, who would be present for the afternoon session.

He explained that the conference would focus on the problems of access to *a school* higher education — and not just physical access. It was important to find out what was being done, and what could be done in the future, to make it easier for people with disablement to participate. In the planning of the meeting, one of the themes that had come through time and again was the difficulty posed by the fragmentation of the sources of financial provision, and he hoped this would receive wider discussion during the day.

Professor Smith concluded by saying that the Open University was most grateful to a variety of very generous sponsors, whose support for the conference had proved essential. They were (in alphabetical order):

CIBA GEIGY LIMITED; THE ESSO PETROLEUM COMPANY; FERRANTI LIMITED; MARKS AND SPENCER LIMITED; THE MULTIPLE SCLEROSIS SOCIETY; THE POSSUM RESEARCH FOUNDATION; RACAL ELECTRONICS LIMITED; ROWNTREE MACKINTOSH LIMITED; SHELL (UK) and the VANESSA LOWNDES CHARITABLE TRUST. One sponsor wished to remain anonymous.

He then called upon the first speaker, Professor Marsland.

The disabled student at a large civic university

E.A.MARSLAND

(Pro-Vice-Chancellor, Vice-Principal and Chairman of Committee on Disabled Members of the University, University of Birmingham)

Introduction

After the Second World War, the universities were faced with the tasks of making good the losses of the period of conflict and meeting the new needs of the post-war era. Their available resources in terms of buildings, equipment and manpower were very limited. This left them with little margin to consider and provide for the needs of minority groups such as the physically handicapped.

Throughout this post-war period, however, there had been developing concern over the quality of life and opportunity for the disabled and—whereas many of the services supplied initially by the welfare state were concerned with aids and social amenities—it was inevitable that the attention would be turned to aspects such as education and employment. The demands the physically handicapped made for their rightful place in the world directed attention to the intellectual capacities that many of them had and, perhaps for the first time, universities—through the Committee of Vice-Chancellors and Principals and the University Grants Committee—began to give some consideration to the voices that were raised.

The major stimulus to development was without any doubt the Chronically Sick and Disabled Persons Act of 1970, which appeared, rather fortuitously, at a time when universities were recovering from the world-wide student unrest that had characterized the late sixties. This unrest, as many of us know, produced a call by students to become involved in the management of the universities of which they were a part, and it was encouraging that disabled young people became more insistent in their demand for access to higher education in all its forms. In the case of my own University—and whilst I am not here to eulogize Birmingham, I must talk about it since it is the only University I know very much of—the Vice-Chancellor asked me to look at the provision that we might make for those with physical handicap, and, at the same time, readily agreed to the establishment of a joint committee of Council and Senate, charged with the specific task of examining our policies in relation to the disabled, and doing what was feasible to make our faculties accessible on a campus composed of a mix of old and new buildings.

The Committee on Disabled Members of the University

The experience we have gained at Birmingham indicates that there are very many advantages in having a committee exclusively devoted to the needs of disabled staff and students. In Birmingham's case, it is the more effective for being kept small. It comprises disabled and able-bodied members of academic staff, a moderately handicapped lay member of Council and three students from the Guild of Students Welfare Committee, who are in some years, to their regret, all able-bodied but on occasions have included disabled undergraduates. Also on the Committee, as one would expect, is the Tutor to Disabled Students, and we have in attendance the University Medical Officer, the Welfare and Lodgings Officer and representatives from the Estates and Buildings Office.

All matters relating to the welfare and the provision of facilities for the handicapped are considered by the Committee. In its early days, its major concerns were access to our buildings, the provision of wheelchair routes across the campus and the installation of toilets suitable for the disabled in what we defined as the priority areas. I dealt first with crucial buildings, such as the main Library, the Students Union and the Hall of Residence geographically closest to the main campus. An annual allocation of money from the Minor Works Budget has been made to the Committee since it started work and, even in the increasingly difficult years since 1975, the University has maintained the level of financial support necessary to the continuing programme of alterations that has been defined.

The operation of the Committee has been helped by having as its chairman a senior member of staff, latterly a Pro-Vice-Chancellor. The result of this is that the disabled members of the University have a spokesman on the higher committees of the University and I see this, I must confess from personal experience, as very important indeed. It is essential to have that input at the highest possible level. The Pro-Vice-Chancellor concerned is in a position to remind those responsible for the allocation of money and the organization of Minor Works of the University's obligations to its physically handicapped members.

In considering the allocation of its financial resources, the Committee on Disabled Members follows two general lines of policy. The first is to devote some part of the budget to the provision of general facilities on the campus and, in parking this year, for example, priority is being given to installing an appreciable number of kerb cut-outs, which will provide easier movement around the campus to those in wheelchairs and will give more direct routes. Could I just add a comment here which seems to me to be very important. What we have done on the campus for the disabled and those in wheelchairs has been greeted enthusiastically by the porters on our campus who have to wheel trolleys around and, I think, this is a point that needs emphasizing whenever we think about planning for the disabled. The Committee has found that much of what we do on behalf of the disabled is every bit as welcome to the able-bodied.

And I would like to quote another example; we have installed in the main corridor of the University a ramp and, although the University will deny it, it was installed so that I could get to my office and there might be some pretence that they were getting some work out of me. That main corridor was used by half the staff of the University. I have not had time to stand at the top and do a survey, but 85 per cent of my able-bodied colleagues walk up and down the ramp in preference to going down the steps. If you look in our accident book, the greatest number of man-hours lost is through slipping down steps and stairs. We haven't lost a single man-hour through slipping on a ramp. The disabled are helping the abled bodied to the sort of provision they should have insisted on years ago.

The second part of the allocation is held in reserve in order to provide facilities to meet the needs of individual disabled students or members of staff. An example here is the provision of a ramp in our Department of Physics for a member of staff now quite severely disabled by multiple sclerosis. It has also been necessary in his case to install, at appreciable cost, a suitable toilet close to his office.

As well as concerning itself with physical facilities on the campus, the Committee, through its members, has been able to influence the attitude of the faculties in the University towards the admission of disabled students, but some showed initial reluctance to consider the physically handicapped. There is still resistance, perhaps understandably, in some areas such as Organic Chemistry, where there are serious risks, and some other science disciplines such as Mechanical Engineering; but the insistent enthusiasm of the Committee has done much to persuade faculties to admit disabled students in the knowledge that any problems that may arise can be referred to the Committee and that solutions will be found without demands being made on either faculty or departmental financial resources.

Ten years of experience indicates the value of a committee charged with direct responsibility for the disabled on the campus. Much has been achieved by the concerted efforts of a small number of deeply involved individuals combining to form an active committee that approaches its work responsibly, and whose recommendations are, therefore, accepted widely throughout the University. It is also a useful source of expert advice to other committees of the University, e.g. those generally responsible for safety matters, such as the evacuation of members of staff and students.

Academic considerations

There is no more challenging point to debate than the question of whether positive discrimination should be operated when consideration is being given to the admission of disabled students. Positive discrimination in respect of provision of accommodation, concessions with examination procedures and perhaps priority in meal queues will be widely acclaimed; but it can be argued that the disabled, who complain of treatment as second-class citizens, will themselves help to perpetuate that attitude if they seek concessions where they can be expected to compete on an equal basis, that is on the grounds of intellectual capacity. There is here a general point with wider implications because—in this International Year, when the disabled are intensifying their efforts to achieve integration and recognition as contributing members of society—the question has to be posed, can the disabled at the same time obtain concessions which give them preference and might, in the eyes of some, make them more privileged members of the community? Here arises the exercise of a fine control, which had to be fully considered at Birmingham University. The policy that emerged is that the academic factors relating to disabled students are kept entirely separate from the work of the Committee that I have mentioned. Applications from physically handicapped students are processed in the normal way through Admissions Tutors in our faculties, schools and departments, and no attempt is made at any stage to persuade those colleagues to adjust entry requirements on the grounds of disability. All Admissions Tutors are made aware that the Chairman and the Tutor for Disabled Students are both available to give guidance on any specific points arising from the handicap, but our Admissions Tutors would rightly resent intervention on behalf of a disabled applicant by a colleague with little or no knowledge of the discipline concerned.

It is important that disabled students do not enter a course with any feeling that they are intellectual inferiors of the other students in the year, and it is equally important that their teachers do not lower academic standards for those with handicaps, and bring the quality of the degree into disrepute.

Admission procedures

Admission Tutors are requested to forward to the Chairman of the Committee on Disabled Members of the University and to the Tutor for Disabled Students, copies of all UCCA forms received from disabled applicants, whether or not they are to be further considered for admission. The Registry files all forms received in order to establish an expanding bank of information on all applicants who will in the future be the subject of follow-up exercises, whether or not they gained entrance to the University. In the second stage of the admissions procedure, the names of applicants selected for interview are notified concurrently to the Chairman of the Committee, the Tutor and the University Medical Officer and, following the academic part of the interview, the opportunity is taken of discussing with the applicant any special facilities that may be required if he or she gains admission to the University. This is regarded as a very important element in the procedure, for it gives advance notice of the need for structural alterations, ramps, handrails, special toilets, etc. Such alterations will proceed to a planning stage, although no work will be commissioned until it is known later in the year whether the student concerned will in fact be entering the University. In this way, we avoid the risk of undertaking inadequately planned alterations in a rush at the beginning of the session when the particular student arrives. Consideration can also be given to the needs of those with sensory handicaps, and they can be made aware of certain items of special equipment that are already available and they can be asked about any other items that they might need. If they do need something, this is the time to come to our Equipment Committee with a request for more money. It is also helpful to find out whether there will be need for an input from Community Service Volunteers, Social Services Departments or a call for readers for any blind students. The interview with the Medical Officer is, of course, confidential, but it does define any special nursing or care needs that there may be and, without in any way breaching the confidentiality, the Chairman of the Committee and the Medical Officer cooperate in ensuring that any joint services that may be essential for a disabled student are available at the start of the session.

In the event of any remaining uncertainty, the Chairman or the Tutor will follow up the interview either by telephone or in correspondence in order to ensure that the inevitably difficult early days at the University proceed as smoothly as possible. The transition to university life for all undergraduates is not easy and it can be made much more troublesome for those with handicaps if adequate forward planning is not undertaken.

The third stage of the procedure is initiated at the time when it is known that a particular disabled student is definitely coming to the University. Any structural alterations that are required are then put in hand and contact made with the service agencies that will be involved with the welfare of the individual in order to confirm their availability on the first day of the term. At this stage also, further discussions are held with the Warden of the Hall of Residence involved, in order again to outline any special needs that a student may have and to alert resident members of the Senior and Junior Common Room of the arrival of another student who may need help from them. In our institution students, of course, are not expected to provide help with care unless they wish to do so of their own volition, and it has to be said that there has been some resentment among some students when disabled students themselves have anticipated too much in the way of assistance from their able-bodied peers. A further facet of this stage of the admissions procedure is to seek, in the case of severely handicapped applicants, the guidance of a local social rehabilitation unit run by our Social Services Department. The rehabilitation officers in this Unit have in the past been extremely helpful in assisting severely handicapped students to independence in the activities of daily living and thus enabling them to play a fuller part in the academic and social activities concerned with both the University and the Hall of Residence. It is not the function of a university to undertake rehabilitation, but it is rewarding to be involved in a programme of work that leads to a higher level of independence with the possibility of a widening range of career opportunities in post-university days.

It has, however, to be admitted that not all the problems connected with disabled applicants can be solved. A severely handicapped student may not have the capacity to fulfil course obligations that include field work or other practicals requiring high levels of mobility, e.g. degrees in archaeology, geology, civil engineering. In some instances it has been possible to adopt a scheme that enables the disabled student to undertake a limited range of practical tasks by becoming part of a team but, where training in individual skill is essential, there may be no solution to the problems that are raised.

Demand

In the ways that have been outlined, a large civic university has progressively provided, at appreciable cost to the taxpayer, the facilities which now enable it to welcome applications from those with severe physical handicap. The University is committed, through its Council and Senate, to a positive policy as far as the disabled student is concerned and, in a time of ever increasing financial difficulty, has made a not ungenerous allocation of resources on behalf of this group of students. Over the last ten years there has been an increase in the number of applications received from disabled students and in the number admitted, but some academic colleagues have questioned the whereabouts of the numbers of disabled students for whom these quite expensive facilities have been created. Demand has not risen in the way that the Committee would have wished, neither, with regret, do large enough numbers of disabled applicants attain the A level grades forecast by their schools and colleges. Subjective optimism on the part of college tutors may well lead, at the end of perhaps many years of hard struggle, to deep and damaging disappointment if the A levels attained do not open University doors.

The future

Attempts to assess the future prospects for disabled students at our well-established civic universities are fraught with the same uncertainties that today confront all areas of university activity. The economies that are to be imposed as a result of the government cuts in expenditure will 'dis-able' provision for the disadvantaged and, in order to ensure that the disabled are not deprived of their right to enter universities, there is need to examine the way in which the appropriate facilities are distributed nationally. Despite the demands of the Chronically Sick and Disabled Persons Act, is it soundly based policy, in times of economic stringency, to expect all 45 of our universities to make provision for the small number of impaired students likely to arrive at any individual institution? It is impossible to obtain accurate figures on the number of disabled students at university for, despite the requests to provide information on the UCCA form, prospective students with hidden disabilities may not wish to declare them, and there are young people with mobility problems who would resent being classified as disabled. Analysing such evidence as is available, and trying to anticipate how demand may rise, the forecasts are that the maximum number of disabled likely to seek entrance to a university in any one year is 450-500. Not all of these will need the facilities and alterations that are necessary for the severely handicapped, but, even if this figure is accepted without reservation, it would mean no more than a small number of severely disabled students at each university. These small numbers result in the slow accumulation of expertise and experience in dealing with the problems and, although the philosophy of giving the disabled applicant the same range of choice as the able-bodied has much to commend it, it may be argued that it would be in the best interests of the disabled if the facilities that they need are concentrated in strength at a limited number of universities, rather than spread thinly but evenly across all.

DISCUSSION

Mr Paul Chennell, University of St Andrews, asked Professor Marsland whether concentrating disabled students in a smaller number of universities would not lead to choice being made on the grounds of the facilities available, rather than on the more desirable academic criteria. Where a university had a high reputation in a particular subject, he felt it most important that a disabled person should have the opportunity of studying there, even though this might mean *all* universities having to make some sort of provision for them.

Professor Marsland replied that it was a difficult point especially as we knew so little about the future of the universities over the next few years with regard to resources and the amount of central direction. He felt that *all* students might be faced with much less choice than in the past and, although he would like disabled students to have exactly the same choice as the able-bodied, he doubted whether every university would in fact be able to offer adequate peripheral and daily living support. This argument really applied mainly to the severely handicapped, perhaps in wheelchairs and needing staff support, and where there were, in fact, limitations on their academic choice because of the physical arrangements and resources of different campuses. There were campuses where he frankly felt it would be unwise for anyone in a wheelchair to go.

Dr John Horlock, Open University, said that he had come from a small civic university where the approach was to make provision for the disabled in the Students' Union and some Halls of Residence, and then to say that only in particular subjects could provision be made for disabled students. On a similar basis it might be possible to make a list in the UCCA booklet in which all universities made it clear in which subjects they could provide for disabled students.

Professor Marsland thought that this might be a helpful proposal. In his own university for example, it was virtually impossible to get wheelchairs in and out of the Law Faculty. Such a list of courses, faculties, departments, and facilities available would be a long one, and offer a very considerable range of choice.

Lord Snowdon said he spoke with some trepidation, as he had never completed his final examinations in architecture, and therefore was still perhaps an undergraduate; nevertheless, he felt there was a case for being extremely critical of the work of certain architects who, even in the Year of Disabled People, were designing for the disabled as an afterthought, with results that were often both expensive and ineffective. Examples were to be found not only in universities, but also in the National Theatre, and in streets with a ramp for the disabled on one side of the road but not the other (so that people could get half way across and would then have to turn back), in the provision of lavatories for the disabled at the bottom of a flight of steps, and so on.

Fire precautions were often used as an excuse to exclude the disabled. He had heard only the previous day that a major company would not allow an unaccompanied blind person into any of its cinemas; he considered that this was an absolute disgrace.

On a more personal note, Lord Snowdon also mentioned that as from 1982 the National Fund for Research into Crippling Diseases would be operating what was being called the Snowdon Award Scheme, to provide small bursaries for the further education of disabled students.

The disabled student and the Open University

RICHARD TOMLINSON

(Adviser on the Education of Disabled Students, Open University)

The Open University background

The Open University has 69,000 students spread throughout the United Kingdom. They have a range of 151 courses available for study. There are 3,519 disabled students registered with the University and 1,633 of them are at present enrolled on courses. That is 2.4 per cent of the total student population. Disabled students too have the same range of courses available. They too are spread throughout the United Kingdom. I state these facts to show that the Open University is seen as a major provider of higher education for disabled people, and also to make the point that disabled students are viewed primarily as students. There are, for example, no courses specifically for disabled students.

There is a range of support services available. These are coordinated in the Disabled Students Office at Walton Hall and can be initiated from there or from any of the thirteen regions, from the Students Association or, indeed, from statutory or voluntary bodies outside the University. The support services are not provided for students alone. A substantial effort is put into providing information, guidance and advice to staff, both full time and part time, who are actually meeting, teaching and counselling students in the Regions, and also to the course teams at Walton who are writing the material for study.

I should like to describe two of the services available in slightly more detail and point out some of the problems as well as the advantages.

The University supplies learning material in a variety of forms. There is television, radio, home experiment kits, cassettes and records, but primarily there is the written word. A full credit course, for example, is divided into 32 Units of written work. Each Unit comprises about 40 pages—1,280 pages in all, for each full credit course. In addition, there are set books, supplementary material and recommended readings. For a person who cannot see, this presents a considerable obstacle. There are at present 169 students identified as having visual impairment. How do they study? The University, in conjunction with the Royal National Institute for the Blind, has taken upon itself the responsibility for reproducing all course material on cassette tape. This medium was preferred as it allows access to the many students who do not read braille, is relatively cheap and easy to duplicate, does not require very precise skills by the reader—most people can operate a tape recorder and read material into it. This task has now nearly been completed. However, it would be an oversimplification to say that blind students' problems are at an end. The transference from one medium to another is not a straightforward operation. There are continuous problems, as to how graphs and diagrams should be described, whether comments should be made on illustrations, how mathematical formulae are named, whether footnotes should be included in the main text or left to the end of the chapter. So volunteer readers have to acquire some expertise, as do blind students, in coming to grips with the various conventions. The problems are also technical. One major disadvantage of learning from tape is not being able to flick through material, nor to refer back quickly and easily to previous material. There needs to be an indexing system, either of bleeps on the tape, or the spoken voice recorded at far higher speed, in the background. We have not adequately solved this problem yet.

This brief illustration highlights many of the features common to the University's services to disabled students. They are general and low level. A student may still have to organize a network of personal support at home. He or she might get assistance from the local branch of the Students Association and the Regional Office or statutory or voluntary bodies, but even so might still require more specific assistance from a member of the family, a neighbour or a friend.

Another service reinforces these points: advice and guidance notes to part-time members of staff. There are over 5,000 part-time members of staff in the Regions. The majority will have little or no experience of students who are handicapped. If they do have some experience, it tends to be restricted to one or two students at the most. It can come as a surprise and even a shock to realize that one of your students is deaf and you have no idea how to surmount the communication problems. To offset this to some extent, we publish guidance notes giving some background on, at the moment, twelve disabling conditions and offering comment on the educational implications. We draw on the expertise of our own staff, external consultants and, of course, students for the writing of these.

I shall take notes on hearing-impaired students as an example. They are quite deliberately divided in two: one part for the students and one for the tutor. We actually send both these sections to all hearing-impaired students on request, as we feel they can be used to introduce the specific problems when the student first meets the tutor. Some of the advice is commonsensical but nevertheless bears emphasis, such as not turning away from a deaf student when talking to him or her, or being conscious of the light, other sections deal with a description of different levels of hearing loss and comments on communication techniques available. We are providing a general service. We cannot force people to use it, to read the notes or to come to day schools. However, they are there if required.

In addition to this service, there is a follow-up to the guidance notes in the form of day schools held in the regions, which are attended by both hearing-impaired students and part-time members of staff. At these we can demonstrate equipment as well as encourage continuing students to discuss their experiences with new students.

This has, perhaps, made them wary of divulging too much information. Other people whose disability is only slowly becoming marked, such as partial sightedness or hearing loss, may be unwilling to admit that they are having problems. It thus can be difficult to extract information from disabled applicants to the University. Now some might argue that it is none of our business and, in some instances, this might well be true but, in others, unless we know and can make appropriate preparation, not only can the student have a very unhappy time but so can administrators and tutors. Summer School is just one example where advance information can allow a student, no matter what his or her disability, to enjoy and benefit from the course. Where there is no information, a student in a wheelchair can arrive at a campus that is totally inaccessible and can be confined to a study bedroom for the duration. I should explain that many courses have a one-week residential summer school component which is sited at a conventional university. So, the University encourages disabled students to give information about any problems. This, if anything, allows for positive, rather than negative, discrimination, because it allows us to provide support at the appropriate time. This, and other essential education services, come at no extra cost to the student.

Personnel

The Open University has created an atmosphere whereby not only are disabled students tolerated, their active participation is encouraged. To quote the University policy statement: 'to take all possible practicable steps to enable full participation by disabled students in all aspects of University life'. Much of the responsibility for this is due to the positive attitudes of part-time members of staff in the Regions. As I have said, many will have had no experience but, provided they are prepared to look for information and support, many of the problems can be minimized. Expertise is not necessarily essential to keeping disabled students from dropping out from courses; a positive attitude very often is. The University has appointed a full-time Adviser for Disabled Students at Walton Hall. This is an academic post. The level of appointment is important because it allows negotiations with course teams and regional colleagues to be conducted as equals. The Adviser can become a member of any committee and represent disabled students' interests at Senate and at Advisory Council levels. The University also recognizes its responsibility to disabled students by the appointment of three administrators to implement services, and the creation of the Disabled Students Committee which has representation from all faculties, the Regions, the Students Association and the BBC. The full-time nature of all the posts mentioned is important. This does not necessarily relate to the numbers of students who are disabled, but it does relate to the needs of students. One blind student taking one course can present considerable problems. However, if those problems are resolved, that course becomes accessible to other blind students. The time taken to resolve those problems is not necessarily less because there is only one as compared with ten students taking that course. The Open University is perhaps fortunate in this respect, in that it can play the numbers game impressively, and yet this is only a game, and should be recognized as such by planners, administrators and education authorities. What we are attempting to do here is to meet student need and not congratulate ourselves on the numbers of disabled students enrolled. That need is as great for the student whether he or she be the only one in a University or part of a substantial body of people. It is very difficult for a member of staff whose responsibilities are only part time for disabled students to acquire the experience and the information to respond effectively to the needs

Flexibility

The University expects one academic standard from all its students. No disabled student will get a B.A. (Disabled). However, this does not mean that the University has to be administratively inflexible in attaining the objective of a degree. What matters is that the work is good enough. So assignments can be accepted type written, taped or even, on rare occasions, in braille. Examination papers can be set in a similar range of media. Where assignments present particular difficulties—such as an art question to a blind student—alternatives

15

of similarly demanding material can be set. Extra time can be granted for the submission of assignments, extra home-based tutorials are available, as is telephone teaching. Extra time at exams perhaps presents one of the biggest problems, as it is almost impossible to ascertain how disability will affect speed. There are guidelines available that offer a systematic base for the assignment of extra time and this is a step in ensuring comparability across the country, but they are only guidelines. In the final analysis it is very much up to the student and the relevant member of regional staff to discuss the realistic requirements, on the understanding that no disabled student would wish to think that the examination experience was a softer touch than experienced by his or her able-bodied colleagues.

The integration-segregation debate

Much is made of the need to integrate disabled students into the mainstream of education. The methods by which this can be done provoke heated discussion. By making allowances available to disabled students, I believe that the Open University—almost by accident—has made a major contribution to the cause of integration. All students share a common experience in the course work. They come up against the same academic problems, they have the same likes and dislikes, triumphs and disasters. It is very encouraging to be part of a study group in a study centre, or of a discussion at summer school, in which there is a disabled student. The content of those debates is always the course material, how exciting it is, or appalling, how the tutor does or does not understand the particular academic problem, how encouraging or depressing it is to receive one mark or another for an assignment. In other words, the conversation is very normal, and the fact of a disabled person's presence has no bearing on that discussion. He or she is able to contribute as another student. The whole aim of services for disabled students is so that they can be part of the general life and not set aside and treated as uniquely different.

Research

There are specific research projects, some of which I have hinted at. For example, the problem of indexing tape material after the recording has been made. There are exciting technological innovations, some of which are on display here, such as the microcomputer linked to a synthetic speech output, and the Cyclops system. But I think there are other areas that are even more important but much harder to pin down. I have already outlined some of the ways that the University disseminates its material and pointed to the problems of visually impaired students in having access to the written word. It does seem to me that those students using tapes as a learning medium have an experience that has huge potential for people interested in exploring all the different ways in which people can study. Here we have a core of over 150 people with practical knowledge on the use of tapes for learning. For an institution such as this, that must have an importance. Until now the written word has been the major contributor to the Open University material. Who is to say that that will be so in ten years' time? Will not a student be buying a TV adaptation that plugs him or her into a course team when he or she enrols at the University? Who knows? But I am conscious of the fact that the experience of disabled students now—and the developments that are taking place in technology—are not peripheral to the way that teaching and learning techniques change. They are central, and I feel that this has to be recognized not only within this University, but in education in general.

Conclusion

I have attempted to describe some of the services the Open University offers and to outline the philosophy behind these services. I have commented on some of the general conclusions that we have reached that may have application outside this University. Finally, I should like to reinforce the point that I believe services for disabled students are not an appendage to the mainstream of education but that they are central and, indeed, should be seen as having the potential to pioneer education developments for all students.

DISCUSSION

*Mr. W. Paton, University of Strathclyde,*asked whether the very existence of the Open University might not provide a great temptation to regard it as a kind of dumping ground for disabled students. He felt that in times of economic harassment, if the universities were saying they could not really cope with disabled students, there might be a great temptation for advisers of young people and the schools themselves simply to say that 'the Open University is there,' and dump them. Although he was very impressed by the efforts that the Open University was making, and expressed the hope that they would give 'some of their expertise to the rest of us eventually', he remained a little worried that the Open University might in fact defeat the very object of the Conference.

Mr Richard Tomlinson replied that, while he was conscious of the points made, there were factors which precluded the Open University from 'creaming off — or being a dumping ground for — disabled students. One was that Open University students had to be over 21, with very occasional exceptions (currently perhaps there were less than a dozen disabled students under 21). Therefore, adults, rather than the conventional university population, were being discussed. The other factor was that, although it was not written policy, any young person applying to the Open University was strongly encouraged to explore conventional universities first. Of course, young people often lacked the A levels needed for a conventional university, whereas the Open University did not have entry requirements, simply 'first come, first served'. At present, there would undoubtedly be disabled students at the Open University who had failed to get into a conventional university. Nevertheless, the point was accepted that there were real risks of the sort mentioned.

Mr George Henshaw, Manchester Polytechnic, felt that disabled students who came to the polytechnic were, on average, one or two years older than most other students anyway, so part of the argument was invalid.

Dr E.G. Cantrell, Southampton University, expressed worry about the discrepancy in figures between Professor Marsland's estimate of 400–500 needing higher education each year, and the Open University's estimate of 3,500. He wondered whether the Open University was using a much lower threshold of what constituted disability, or were considering a totally different age group.

Mr Richard Tomlinson replied that he thought the latter was true — a breakdown by age showed a significant weighting towards those in middle age.

Professor Marsland agreed. The figures he had quoted concerned projections on numbers in the normal university age group.

Dr H.W. Gardner, Stirling University, said that his University was designed from the beginning so that it could handle handicapped students. Disabled students were monitored all the way through the University. About 2 per cent of students each year were disabled. The speaker thought that there were probably more disabled people at university than was generally realized. Since monitoring of disabled students at Stirling was from the point of view of those whose work would be fundamentally affected in some way by their disablement, it covered a wide range of disablement.

A graduate's viewpoint

N. SHABAN

I think I have the easiest job of all the speakers, because mine is a graduate viewpoint and has to be fairly specific. I went to a conventional university, Surrey University, and graduated just under two years ago. I am 28 now, so I am in fact older than the normal student who goes to the conventional university.

The reason for my late starting is because it was never expected that I would go to university (this, I believe, is one of the main problems with regard to the statistics of possible demand). The majority of disabled people are just not expected to go into higher education. Their parents don't expect it; if they go to a special school, the school certainly doesn't expect it; and Careers Officers and Disabled Resettlement Officers tend not to expect it either. So, throughout a disabled person's life, especially if he is born disabled, he or she considers it almost unimaginable to be going to university or polytechnic.

I went from a special school, with two CSEs in English and Art. They were, in fact, going to give me an extra CSE to do, in maths, but they didn't want to stretch me too far. So I left school with two CSEs and went to a sheltered workshop for three years. Now I always knew what I wanted to do—O levels, even A levels, and possibly become a professor; and I knew that I could do it, but the school didn't think I could, and the people in the sheltered workshop certainly didn't think I could .

And I pressed all the time while I was at the sheltered workshop, 'Look, one of the reasons I came here was that you promised me the opportunity to do GCEs at a local Technical College'. After six months of nagging, the Superintendent turned round and said 'Look, if you were meant to do GCE O levels and A levels, you would not have been sent here'. So, for three years, I remained in that sheltered workshop. Eventually I managed to get out with a Certificate in Office Studies, not from the sheltered workshop, but from a tech where I went on one day a week. I next managed to go to Hereward College in Coventry, where I did OND in Business Studies.

Again, I had not really believed in the possibility of my going to university, and I was lowering my horizons by considering taking an HND in Business Studies. It was after about a year at Hereward College that the magic word was whispered to me, 'university'.

Applying for university

So then I started to apply. Now the business of applying, when you're a disabled person, is not as straightforward as it is for able-bodied people. Normally, able-bodied potential applicants look at the course, the subjects that interest them, and possibly the locality. Some might like York, others might like Edinburgh. For a disabled student, of course, you don't get that kind of choice. (You can guess that I am opposed to the idea of a university for the disabled, or a few select universities around the country that are for disabled students.) In making my choice I had first to go to the Central Council for the Disabled's Handbook and look up universities and polytechnics that had facilities and a campus suitable for a disabled student.

Eventually I came up with a short list of about five or six, and then I started to look at what courses they had to offer. Because I had been brought up to believe that a disabled person must always be looking for potential career prospects and must not waste valuable resources of the State, must always be considering a degree that would enable him to have a useful career in society, I couldn't go for the more luxurious courses, i.e. philosophy, theology or archaeology. I had to be thinking about studying business or physics or something like that. So I was not looking for a degree that I might enjoy, but a degree that would suit me as a disabled person in society. So, again, that cut down the possibilities.

Having made my choice, I eventually came up with four universities that I could go to, and three polytechnics. I wasn't actually offered an interview by any of them; I had two outright rejections and two outright acceptances from the universities.

Neither of the two acceptances suggested that I came and had a look at the campus; and what it actually described on paper about a campus isn't necessarily what really exists. So I wrote and asked them if I could come and have a look before I finally said yes or no to either of their offers. It was a good job that I did, because, in the first one, the one I was really thinking of going to, the campus was too widely spread and I wouldn't have been able to get from one lecture theatre to another in time.

Choosing a campus

The other campus was built on the side of a hill, Surrey University. They did send a handbook which said there were all these marvellous ramps all over the place but, when I got there, I found that a lot of these marvellous ramps were in fact alongside the steps and were of the same gradient as the steps. There was just no way that I was going to attempt going down them because I would have ended up more disabled than when I had arrived. There were also some of the amazing ramps, which Lord Snowdon was talking about earlier, where you suddenly go careering down a ramp to find that it ends in steps. However, I opted for that university.

Now, I could have chosen Sussex University, but I didn't want to go there because they had a special unit for disabled students and I actually wanted to get away from disabled students. I have been living with disabled people all my life. Also it was a challenge to go to a university that was not completely designed for disabled people. But the point was made that I had to be physically fit to survive at Surrey University, which was rather odd for a disabled person to have to be.

An interesting point is that, at one of the polytechnics, there was a sandwich course related to industry, but, before I was actually offered a place, I had to give an assurance that I could find an industrial placement about two years later. They wouldn't actually offer me a place until I had it written down on paper from an employer that he would give me work for a year in two years' time. Now that is a ludicrous situation: that a disabled student should have to give such an assurance before he can even be considered as an applicant.

So I went to Surrey University, and I was a good boy and actually wrote down on my UCCA form that I was disabled. It didn't make any difference. Nobody knew that I was disabled apart from the academics. They hadn't passed my form on to the Health Centre or to the accommodation department. So, about a week before I actually arrived to do my course, sheer panic arose, when the Head of the Health Centre, leafing through the forms, suddenly discovered that a disabled student in a wheelchair was coming, and she contacted the accommodation people and found they had put me on the second floor with no lift. This was totally unsuitable so, right at the last minute, there was this frenzy to find me suitable accommodation with wooden ramps, etc.

Thus there was no coordination between the departments. However, they felt that they had learned by their mistake and they came up with the idea, at my suggestion, that perhaps all disabled students should be interviewed, should be considered from the point of view of what services and support they would need, and that in fact they should perhaps stay for two days at the University so that they could get to know it and make up their own mind. A proposal was made to this effect that all potential disabled students should come to the University for two days and perhaps stay in the health sickbay centre and thus be able to find out what would be needed.

I went back to the University a couple of weeks ago and found that they had forgotten all about this proposal. They were in a panic again because they were going to have a disabled student in the next session and were asking my advice about what services and facilities would be needed. Actually, I feel somewhat to blame about this because, although I did get involved in trying to ensure that there was a continuity of services and information with regard to what was available for disabled students, I was too busy living the life of a non-disabled person. I really didn't actually want to get involved in saying 'Look at me, I am disabled and I want you always to take into account my needs', and so I just carried on and, as a result, I tended not to write those handbooks that people suggested I might, and tended not to try to get policy passed through the Union to the Senate.

Problems of access

When I first arrived at the University I did tend to consider problems of the disabled but, eventually, life at University overtook and I started to become a normal human being. Now, one of the things that I had to fight for was access to the library—it was up a spiral staircase. There was a way in, through the goods entrance, and I actually succeeded in getting a copy of the key to allow myself into the library.

Another problem was the bars in the Union building. The upper bar was up a spiral slope, which was quite handy except that the barrels stored there blocked my entry to it; the lower bar was also inaccessible to me. So this meant that I couldn't be your stereotyped boozing student, because I just couldn't get to any of the bars. I happened to mention it, in passing, to the Fire Officer, and it turned out that, in fact, the Union was breaking fire regulations by having barrels on the spiral ramp so, eventually, I was able to get into the Union that way.

Another problem is that at Surrey University, because the Union offices are right downstairs, disabled students cannot really consider going in for Union posts. It so happened, however, that both myself and another chap in a wheelchair attempted to stand as President of the Students Union, and we had to do what no able-bodied candidate had to do—we had to give assurances to the electorate that we would find a way in which we could function without having to go downstairs to the Union offices. That took up a substantial part of our manifestos.

Social aspects of university life

There is another factor that academics tend to forget with regard to study: a student doesn't study in isolation, in a vacuum. He needs the motivation and he needs to stave off fits of depression. Those aspects that are likely to inhibit him from studying are usually social aspects. So it's not just enough to make the academic buildings suitable for the disabled person, but sports facilities, Union facilities, theatre facilities, arts workshop facilities, also have to be accessible, because no one is going to want to be studying 24 hours a day and not have any leisure time to themselves. I certainly felt at times that I was in a prison more than in a university, because I couldn't participate in many of the activities until after a year or two, things started to move. Thus it would be well to remember that the social aspect of the disabled student's life at university is as important as the academic.

Now, another thing that I fought against was the suggestion that one or two floors in the accommodation areas should be converted wholly for disabled wheelchair-type students. I said 'No way, we can't have that'. For a start, they were making an assumption that all disabled people have common interests, are all going to like each other and want to be together—rubbish! Also the corridors in those particular areas were not wide enough to enable two wheelchairs to pass. And also, if you do have these ghettos, you are going to have to employ special staff to tend and help these disabled students and, therefore, there is the risk that the disabled student is going to have to pay extra rent for the additional staff.

Whereas, if you have, say, one or two disabled students on a generally 'able-bodied' floor, you have a lot of volunteer help. That doesn't mean that the disabled students should be expecting help from their able-bodied peers but, normally, the disabled person is able to convey to the able-bodied people that he would just like a bit of help. Actually it comes quite naturally anyway. So I don't think there is a problem there.

Cutbacks and the disabled

I am a bit worried about present trends with regard to the cutbacks as far as the disabled are concerned. One Government Minister has stated that the disabled must learn to tighten their belts along with everybody else. That is a bit cruel really, especially when a lot of the disabled don't have any belts. It's a bit like expecting the starving in the Third World to give up their grain in order for the West to put more money into the nuclear arms race.

I don't think there is any reason whatsoever to cut back in expenditure on the education of the disabled. In fact, more money should be put in so that disabled people can choose to go to any of the 45 universities that exist. Because if you don't enable disabled people to develop what they have got rather than what they have not got, if you find that they have the same amount of intelligence and intellectual capacity as the other people, who are supposed to be able to go to university, and you don't develop that, the disabled will rot in sheltered workshops, they will rot in hospitals for the incurables and the State will in the end be spending far more money to keep those people alive and supported. Thus it is short sightedness on the part of the Government even to be considering cutting back on expenditure that will enable disabled people to be self sufficient, self determining and independent.

DISCUSSION

Dr D.A. Reason, University of Kent, stated that, during his experience as a disabled student, and now a disabled lecturer, he had made a kind of transition from the expectation, held by some, that the disabled student should be the expert who was pressing, who had the knowledge, expertise and determination to alter the social as well as physical environment to meet his needs, to the realization that to be an advisor on handicap and education was a full-time job if it were to be at all effective. Dr Reason hoped that the Conference would see the problem of the university authorities, with their policy of trying to meet the needs of the disabled in a sympathetic manner, which had to be balanced against that of the disabled, with their wish *not* to be seen as disabled, in the sense of being segregated, treated as special, or being considered the experts on the subject.

Mr Shaban felt that disabled students should not always have the burden of being 'the experts' pushed onto them, since they were there, after all, to study. Nevertheless, most agitation had to come from the person who was being discriminated against, and who was suffering from lack of foresight. Ideally there should be a tutor responsible for the disabled, but not someone who was going constantly to harass a disabled person with suggestions that this or that might be needed. Mr Shaban recounted his own experience on arrival at Surrey University, when the first thing suggested to him was that he might need an electric wheelchair. He replied that an electric wheelchair would make him even more disabled through lack of exercise, and felt that this was the kind of extreme one could get by having an institutional disabled advisory service. Nevertheless, he felt that universities and other institutions of higher education should have, as in Birmingham University, a committee responsible for disabled members, since constant vigilance was required to ensure that the situation did not go backwards. On his return to Surrey University, for instance, Mr Shaban found that, through lack of a disabled student to complain, the bookshop had a turnstile at its entrance, and the grocer's shop an extra couple of steps. There had to be some kind of continuity, so that when a disabled person left, services did not fail. The present Vice-President of the Students Union had expressed concern to Mr Shaban that the arrival of a disabled student had brought home to him the need for continuity of services for the disabled after he gave up office as Vice-President.

Professor Marsland replied that he considered it wrong to expect a disabled student to be an advisor, when he might wish simply to be an undergraduate at the university. Remarking on Lord Snowdon's comments on architects, Professor Marsland said that at Birmingham architects were found to be 'broken reeds', having no memory from one occasion to the next as to what had proved right or wrong last time. The campus was, nevertheless, lucky in having two able-bodied members of staff in the Estates and Buildings Department who showed particular interest in provision for the disabled, and would knock on doors if necessary to remind the Professor of the needs of the disabled in new student accommodation, etc. This was a tremendous contribution and showed what could be done.

Mrs Dorothy Whittington, Ulster Polytechnic, said that she was impressed by what had been said by a previous speaker about returning to his earlier institution after two years and finding it back in a state of 'pre-wheel technology'. She felt that some of the problems faced by students were always fairly specific, and that even if a specific problem concerning a disabled student arose only once in ten years, the information should not be lost, as it seemed to be at present. She hoped that the Open University, with its unique experience in having gone right through the academic curriculum looking for ways to help the physically handicapped student, would disseminate that information. At a lower, simpler, and less expensive level, it might be important to raise a register of academic institutions which had dealt with students in a particular discipline with a particular handicap so that it would be possible to refer to another university's way of helping with the problem.

Mrs G. Dayan, Institute of Careers Officers, stated that she identified strongly with the case history related by Mr Shaban. With only a few discretionary awards to give out, she had many clients in the same position. The result was that very few could reach higher education, hence some universities found that they only had two per cent handicapped. Some answer to the question of discretionary awards would have to be found.

In a computer study, Mrs Dayan had found that, out of 300 on her case load, only 20 were able to go to courses when they should all have gone. This was because local education authorities had to pay for further studies when a student had been paid for at a special school; yet discretionary awards were particularly difficult to obtain at the present time. Furthermore, there had been no increase in discretionary awards to match the increase in fees of about a third. Thus she was told that she was taking too much, as as proportion of the discretionary awards available, and many of her clients failed to reach University level.

Professor Smith felt that two important points had been raised by Mrs Dayan. Mr Shaban and Professor Marsland. One was the question of financial provision, which would be dealt with in more detail in the afternoon meeting. The second was the level of education in special schools, which were not geared for academic attainment. The second point was possibly beyond the scope of the Conference, but certainly needed attention.

Professor Marsland thought that special schools started out by imposing the conditions of a second-class citizen. A child in a special school – certainly in Birmingham – went to school later, and left school earlier than everybody else, which discriminated straight away. He could find no explanation of this. Even when children had to be bussed, they could presumably be bussed at normal times. It put a different atmosphere on their whole education straight away, and he thought it one of the reasons why there were not more disabled youngsters coming to university. It was accepted by them when very young that they were second-class and inferior citizens, and this under-expectation often extended to the home. A teacher at a school for the deaf had told him some years ago that they never expected to get any children to university, despite the fact that there were children at the school with the intelligence and intellectual ability required.

Mrs G. Dayan said that some of her clients had been so brainwashed that they were very scared by the suggestion that they might reach university level, and many would take years to be convinced.

Mr A.G. McAllister, Hereward College, took up Mrs Dayan's comments on finance and further education. He found it interesting that so much had been said about the local education authority's difficulty in financing further education. In his own College, fees were £6,250 per annum, but fees in special schools could be between £9,000 and £10,000 per annum. There was, therefore, a situation in which further education for the physically handicapped was being looked at less favourably than education at special schools—the Special Education Service being able to finance high fees for students in the 16–18 range, but the further education side of the same authority sometimes finding it extremely difficult to raise his College's fees of £6,250.

Hereward College, which was responsible for severely physically handicapped young people, had sent an average of nine or ten students on to university over the last seven years. He felt there was a case for a change of attitude in the further education side of some local education authorities.

Mr John Stewart, Association of Disabled Professionals, felt that a logical conclusion to Professor Marsland's argument — that a few universities should be selected as suitable for disabled students — was one university for all disabled students. He was against such an idea, feeling that emphasis must be placed on integration, not segregation, and that disabled people enjoyed the company of able-bodied people as well as others like themselves. A special university would also tend to be downgraded, as were special schools. He believed that we should not want to create a parallel to special education in further education.

Professor Marsland stated that he would oppose 'with every fibre of his being' any suggestion of a university for the disabled. Disabled people were not a defined group, but constituted a microcosm of society, having the same spread of personalities, likes, etc. He felt such a university would be a recipe for disaster, would spell disaster for the individual and the institution, and would not encourage the right sort of staff.

Many centres had to accept the load, and his comment had been misinterpreted. He was suggesting that in difficult times, for financial, geographical, architectural or any other reasons, it would be difficult to make 45 universities conform to the needs of the 1970 Act. It was impossible, for instance, to get a student in a wheelchair into the Faculty of Law at his university. Experience and expertise were gained with numbers, and it was just a question of whether investment should be spread over say 25 rather than 45 universities. There were already limited choices for the able-bodied according to courses covered. Professor Marsland did not feel that this was a parallel with special schools.

Dr Richard Holmes, Open University, expressed the view that young people in general had a difficult time gaining the right combinations of A level grades for particular universities anyway, and if, as had been stated, disabled people found it more difficult than others to get the necessary A level grades, their choices were reduced still further. He feared therefore that reduction in the number of 'available' universities would result in the intake of disabled students being sharply reduced, unless the universities did the very thing Professor Marsland said they should not, that is to allow disabled students entry with lower grades.

Dr Roy Webberley, Open University, had looked through the findings of the 'Opportunities for the Handicapped in Higher Education Conference' held in Stockholm in 1978. He felt that one particular recommendation there focused on a number of issues under discussion — namely, 'to secure optimum performance by the handicapped student, there must be a dynamic continuity of the rehabilitation process throughout the whole period of education including higher education'. He felt that previous conference recommendations should not be forgotten, but should be built upon. It did seem that there was a need for more than an 'UCCA guide to disability facilities in universities'. What was needed was some pattern of advice and a central advisory service, more dynamic than the notion simply of an information centre on facilities.

Mr Paul Chennell, University of St Andrews, felt that a reason against cutting down numbers of universities taking disabled students was that it was also an important part of university life for the whole of the student population to meet and mix with other young people from different backgrounds and to meet minority groups. It was valuable for the average able-bodied young person to meet the disabled, and to encounter their needs. Mr Chennell stated that at his own university, which had about 3,500 undergraduates, there were only known to be about 25 students who were disabled. This, he felt, was an unhealthy situation. Despite the very genuine compassion of the University authorities, there were serious architectural problems for disabled students on the campus. He suggested that all universities should provide for disabled people. Able-bodied students should meet enough disabled students to understand their problems.

Mr Ronald Sturt, National Bureau for Handicapped Students, expressed the view that even if Dr Boyson gave every university and every polytechnic a handsome sum of money, it wouldn't change attitudes. Money would still be spent in the ways it had been spent for the last ten years, and would not provide the improvements suggested today. The changes must come from within. Universities and polytechnics had had plenty of resources over the years, yet we were still faced with minimal activity among staff and other students in creating opportunities for the handicapped.

We should remember that we were getting more handicapped staff in our institutions for various reasons, and he thought that attitudes in Birmingham had changed profoundly as a result of Professor Marsland's appearance there. Members of staff were now letting people know that they had problems which could limit their mobility, but he questioned the suggestion that the problems were mainly concerned with physical access. The majority of problems were not.

Mr Sturt expressed the hope that everyone with a case study would send it to the Bureau where it would be included in a termly publication, thus building up a bank of precedent and good practice. He stated that when he was working at the Bureau he had been worried by lack of coordination in decision taking.

In the first few months, there had been two cases in universities and one in a polytechnic where the academic decision was taken to offer a provisional place, and the later, medical, decision was 'no'. The effect on the students was very bad. He felt that procedures should be looked at to make sure that they were at least coordinated. He asked Professor Marsland if his university's coordination was now at the point where it could guarantee that the student received one comprehensive answer.

Professor Marsland replied that he could only speak for Birmingham, where the University Medical Officer would not be allowed to refuse entry to any disabled student; in these matters his role was advisory. Such a decision was made purely on academic grounds, provided there was the appropriate accommodation, and even that proviso was with regret, because the University would like accommodation for all disabled students however great their handicap. Yet they did not wish to build a special block and were trying to make provision in normal halls of residence and in self-catering accommodation, where only minor adjustments were needed for the disabled student to be part of the cooking group. Providing the academics wanted the student, the whole procedure and decision making was finally passed on to the Chairman of the Committee and the Tutor for the Disabled, who coordinated everybody's information. The Registrar, or Vice-Chancellor, if they received enquiries, passed them to the Committee. The importance of the Committee could not be stressed too strongly. It was no use creating facilities and giving an individual a job unless he was backed by a strong committee that was listened to by the university. The Committee coordinated.

Mr Hans Cohn, speaking as a totally blind person, said that he would like to add his voice to that of Professor Marsland in saying that the last thing a handicapped person wanted was a university for the handicapped. They wanted more integration of education at university level. In fact, the need for integration started as far down as the primary schools.

He hoped that the Vernon Report and the Warnock Report on the education of the handicapped, which spoke of more integration, would result in more policy from government, and from the organizations of, and for, the handicapped towards this end.

Much had been said about the cooperation of the handicapped, but it was not realized by enough people that, in this age of participation, the handicapped of all kinds were getting organized into groups of individual handicaps, and also jointly into organizations. The way to consult the handicapped and to ask them what they actually wanted was not just to consider what other people thought they wanted, or to rely on the advisor or handicapped member of one's own staff, but to realize that organizations of the handicapped, organized on democratic grounds, could be consulted on all kinds of issues. University authorities should realize that the handicapped all over the country were joining self-help organisations, with elected officers able to speak for them.

Miss Jean Birrell explained that the session was devoted to the question of financial provision for disabled students in higher education and hoped that the Conference would be looking at some of the many different types of financial difficulties students were experiencing both in taking up higher education, and, indeed, in getting that far.

She said that the first speaker, Mr Richard Stowell from the National Bureau for Handicapped Students, had taken as the title of his talk 'Is the complexity of financial provision handicapping disabled students?', and that she would ask Mr B. Massie of the Royal Association for Disability and Rehabilitation and then Mr D. Child, Association of Blind and Partially Sighted Teachers and Students to open the general discussion of the issues that Mr Stowell raised.

Is the complexity of financial provision handicapping disabled students?

RICHARD STOWELL

(Director, National Bureau for Handicapped Students)

My brief today is to discuss financial provision for disabled students in higher education and to pose the question, 'Is the complexity of financial provision handicapping disabled students?'. I shall mention later the special provision for the disabled student and also the finance that is available for the personal care of the student and for various aids and equipment. But, first of all, I believe it is necessary to make two points by way of putting the problem into context.

The first point is that we are here, in higher education, discussing only three, maybe four, years of a disabled person's life. There may be some who have experienced traumatic injury shortly before, or during their academic life, but in the great majority of cases we are here talking about people disabled at birth or in early childhood, for whom the problem and complexity of financial provision did not begin when they were accepted for a place in higher education. Nowadays, for example, from the age of two, a severely handicapped child will qualify for an attendance allowance and, at five, for a mobility allowance. Meanwhile, the parents will possibly have received services from the local authority under the Chronically Sick and Disabled Persons Act, and this may have involved a complicated means test. At the time of school leaving, the handicapped young person may well have encountered the dilemma of whether to opt for the Non-Contributory Invalidity Benefit or seek Supplementary Benefit, with all the complexities that that involves, and a mature student will have almost certainly encountered more benefit problems.

We should not lose sight of the fact that one of the main objects of higher education should be to enable the student to overcome the handicap that

31

disability brings and escape a life-long dependence on those welfare benefits by achieving financial independence. But in considering the complexity of financial provision for disabled students, we should not forget that it is but one part of the whole complex system of provision for handicapped people in this country. This system of provision is, in fact, a mixture of confused principles and piecemeal legislation and has been accurately described by Lord Plowden, in an introduction to research commissioned by the Disablement Income Group, as the 'Kafka-like world in which the disabled and handicapped have to exist' (1).

Barriers to the disabled student

The second general point I wish to make before I go on to discuss in detail the provision for the student in higher education, is that the barriers to the disabled student at this level in terms of financial provision are usually as of nothing compared to those to be found in the further education sector.

A question I am commonly asked is 'how many disabled students are there in higher education?' and I think we heard this morning, in truth, there is no ready-made answer to the question. The Government Social Survey published in 1971 suggested that there could be 9 young people per 1,000 between the ages of 16 and 29 with some form of locomotive impairment (2).

A National Innovations Centre report (3) suggests that perhaps only 2 per thousand students in higher education are similarly impaired, although those statistics are a little out of date. Both surveys probably underestimate the numbers of disabled young people but, clearly, disabled students are heavily under-represented in higher education.

There may be a number of reasons for this. Many handicapped young people, particularly the more severely handicapped, will have attended special schools. While there are some advantages in this type of segregated education—not least the high pupil-teacher ratio, and the encouragement to develop physical potential and build up confidence in their abilities—none the less it is often the case that the sheltered atmosphere of some special schools can be a great disadvantage to the pupil who wishes to progress to higher education. As we heard this morning, it is also inevitable that where a large proportion of the day is spent in mobility training and physiotherapy, or where, as often the case, the time taken to transport pupils to school limits the school hours, say from 10 until 3, there will be less time for academic work. Where there is a narrow curriculum or less competition from fellow pupils, the academic standard will tend to suffer, and so often the 'special' school environment becomes too safe and not challenging enough.

32

Lack of expectation

The academically able pupil may also have to overcome a lack of expectation by staff, parents and society at large. In this context it is worth quoting a remark by a Deputy Regional Director of the Open University made of one student. In his report he wrote of the student, 'The student seems to have made a compromise that I would regard as characteristic of many disabled persons. It is not that he is short of needs, so much as short of expectations. He had, I believe, come to terms with a fairly general lack of local authority concern, and limited his efforts to what he can, on the whole, achieve unaided'. I should like to add that the Deputy Director was careful to comment that he was continuing to encourage this student to take a more positive attitude.

Often it is the highly determined and articulate disabled people who will be undeterred by refusal and discrimination. But for every determined and articulate person there are many who fall by the wayside and are likely to be destined for a life of under-achievement.

I would not, however, like to give the impression that things are not improving, they are. Many new and imaginative courses have begun in recent years in the further education sector and a number of link and bridging courses are now designed to equip the handicapped student to move with a feeling of competence from school to further and higher education. Many further education colleges are also now offering a second chance for those whose educational development has been delayed or who wish to retrain having become disabled later in life. It is at the *further* education level that most of the Bureau's work must continue and it is also at this level that the lack of financial provision and the complexity of provision, is at its greatest.

The inadequacy of financial provision

This problem was recognized in the Warnock Report, which spoke of their recommendations for the post-16 education of handicapped young people being of 'little avail' unless adequate financial assistance was made available. Yet a survey of careers officers carried out in 1980 (4) showed that almost half (47%) of the authorities either had some restrictions on the number of handicapped pupils who could remain at school, or had little or no provision, whilst almost three-quarters (74%) were felt to have restricted, or little or no, suitable further education provision for the handicapped. Not only were there problems of inadequate financial provision, but lack of qualified support services and repeated problems of access and mobility for the physically handicapped.

There may be many advantages in placing physically handicapped students in residential colleges, such as Hereward College in Coventry. This, and a number of residential colleges, accept students from all over the country—an essential provision, particularly in cases where local provision is so limited. All the more disturbing then that the overriding view of careers officers—who have to deal with the day to day problems of finding funds—should be one of dissatisfaction with the present system of discretionary awards and the inequities that result.

I echo the view of one careers officer who wrote, 'The situation is too piecemeal. Local education authority grants, Training Service Division finance and DHSS allowances all operate independently from one region to another. There is a desperate need for coordination and standardization', to which I would add there is also a desperate need for more finance.

In one local education authority—as it happens one of the better authorities—a special careers officer told me that last year, and this might sound familiar, from a total of 300 handicapped young people who, in her view, should benefit from further education, she was able to find funding for just 20. It is no wonder that careers officers have to scratch around for finance, or that desperate efforts are made to extract benefit from schemes—and I am thinking particularly of Manpower Services Commission (MSC) schemes—which were never designed with the special needs of handicapped people in mind. And so we have arguments about whether a course is chiefly a training course—in which case the MSC must pay, or largely educational—in which case the education authority must assume responsibility. There are arguments too about whether the handicapped young person is there for educational purposes—receiving an education grant—or chiefly for social reasons—in which case the social services department must pick up the bill. All time-consuming, costly, and dispiriting arguments, which serve only to reduce further the opportunities available to the handicapped school leaver.

I may have made this point too long and I apologize, but I do feel it is important when we are considering provision for the disabled student in higher education, to understand why it is so few reach the stage even of applying for places in our universities and polytechnics. Having braved the rough seas of further education, few make it through to the relatively safe haven of higher education and to a mandatory award.

The mandatory award system

Such mandatory awards are, of course, means-tested, usually on the parental income, and no account is taken of all the additional expenditure the parents have made over the years for their handicapped child but at least the award is an automatic one. The student no longer has to compete in what is a virtual lottery to decide on his or her future.

There are of course problems even in the mandatory award system (and these need to be borne in mind when we argue for an extension of the mandatory award system to cover the handicapped student in further education). Means-testing is one, but another is the policy of limiting mandatory awards to one course of study, any further award being discretionary. If this were not changed we could see a situation developing where a handicapped person received a mandatory grant to study for O or A level, but then had to compete for a discretionary grant for a degree course with the chances that it could effectively nip a promising career in the bud.

Indeed, this inflexible approach does already handicap some disabled students in higher education. The Bureau has come across a number of cases where students have had, of necessity, to change courses in the middle of their studies. One example I can give is that of a medical student who was diagnosed as having multiple sclerosis and who could not continue with his medical studies but wanted to change to study for a social science degree. Or again, there are students who may become disabled through sudden accident or illness and will often want to resume studies after a period of rehabilitation, but whose new circumstances, and possible uncertainty as to the future, dictate a transfer to another course or discipline.

We see the problem also in the post-graduate sector. One example of the problem is illustrated in the case of a young man, a mild athetoid spastic young man, who was advised on completing his first degree that the only possibilities open to him lay either in a sheltered office job, or an academic outlook. Choosing the academic outlook, he was accepted for an MA course but was told by his local education authority that, when it came to personal care and a grant, he had 'had enough help already, and could not expect any more help'.

It is encouraging to note that more and more institutions these days are opening up their admissions procedures to admit students who may enter higher education as mature students and do not necessarily possess a prescribed qualification. The financial concerns and commitments of a mature student of say 30 are likely to be very different from those of the eighteen-year-old school leaver.

So many disabled students will not have followed a traditional path to tertiary education and it is therefore essential that higher education itself, and the student award scheme, both encompass an element of flexibility.

The mandatory grant, of course, is expected to cover all a student's needs—for food, clothing, accommodation, travel, books, and so on. Whatever one may think about where the priorities for higher student grants may rank in priorities for further public expenditure, there will be few who will say that the current size of student grants allows for a very comfortable style of living. But part of a student's life surely is living cheaply, in inexpensive accommodation, hitchhiking where necessary, and working in vacation jobs to augment the low grant.

Extra costs

Consider, if you will, the position of the disabled student. Such a student will often need larger, well-heated accommodation and, in any case, the cheap accommodation in most of our cities tends to be in older buildings which tend to be inaccessible for the wheelchair student. I know of a student who has hitchhiked from a wheelchair, but I don't think even he would recommend it. Meanwhile the vacation jobs are usually unskilled manual activities, not necessarily easily obtainable or the best type of job for a disabled student.

But, in addition, and this is an important point, most or all disabled people generally face *extra* costs as a result of their disability, costs which do not suddenly disappear when a student enters the academic setting. Clothes do not wear out any slower on wheelchairs and calipers, cheap supermarkets do not suddenly become accessible, or extra heating any less necessary the moment a disabled person puts on a college scarf. These extra costs, research by the Disablement Income Group has shown, can easily amount to 25% of all expenditure (5).

Clearly, there are some authorities who appear to pay automatically the full amount, or who will give individual consideration to each case, but will normally pay close to the maximum and we must applaud these education authorities. Equally, however, there are others who interpret the regulations such that they will only use the allowance for large items of educational equipment, and will not use it to compensate the disabled student for extra living cost. There are others who claim never to have received requests for help, or admit to offering assistance only when the DHSS will no longer help. It does not require much thought to imagine the arguments that ensue between different departments when, to take one example, a muscular dystrophy student whose mother had previously had the task of turning him over in bed every night, found that among other things, he required a self-turning bed possibly costing £225, in order that he could leave home and get to university.

I can report, however, that after representations from the Bureau, the DES have made a commitment to look carefully during the course of the next grant review at whether or not the disabled person's living allowance should be made a mandatory element.

As always in the disability world, there will be individuals in some local authorities who will ensure that the disabled student knows about and receives all the help that is available, but equally there will be many cases where students will be in ignorance of their entitlement. It really does show how we need the Warnock concept of the 'named person' to be put into practice! However, the DES have accepted that a fairer and more consistent approach is required and have made a commitment to the Bureau that they will issue a circular letter to all education authorities reminding them of their responsibilities, and will also be considering a phased enhancement of the special allowance. At present, however, there is no organized assessment as to what education aids a student might need.

We recently organized an assessment for one university student with cerebral palsy, who was recommended to purchase a Microwriter, costing in excess of £1000, in order to take lecture notes. In such circumstances, the maximum allowance of £235 appears woefully inadequate and we are left with the slightly unedifying sight in some cases of college administrations and student unions scratching around for the funds to purchase an essential piece of equipment.

Even when the £235 grant covers the cost of an aid, it is often given without the appearance of good grace. One can understand why local education authorities, given the responsibility of administering something they know little about, resort to demanding bills and receipts as they would of contractors, but it really is nonsense to expect students to account for every penny in this way, as if every disabled was out to make a fast buck.

The difficulty of quantifying costs

Of course, having to account for every penny excludes the possibility of claiming for costs which are not easily quantifiable. It is a daunting, if not impossible task to list all the extra costs he is incurring. A few examples here will suffice:

The hearing-impaired student, for example, more reliant on the written word, may need to purchase more books.

The visually handicapped student will need to make more use of the telephone.

The physically handicapped student will often need to make more use of photocopiers.

It would certainly be an imposition, if not an impossibility, to have to provide written proof of each element of this additional expenditure, let alone proof of extra heating, clothing or dietary costs.

The same principle applies to travel costs. Where the travelling costs of the disabled student have been necessarily incurred for a course, the education authority must reimburse the full amount, but who is to say what travel is necessarily incurred?.

For someone very severely disabled, however, the major additional expenditure may come in the form of needing help with personal care. In 1976 Dr Gunn of Reading University found that, among those universities he contacted, only two took on extra nursing services to facilitate the stay of physically handicapped students. Ten other institutions made use of the District or Domiciliary nursing staff, and only four had students in residence with full-time attendants. There are problems enough coordinating the various services but, whatever form of personal care is needed, the task of securing financial provision is rarely a simple one.

In most cases the home social services department will accept responsibility for the student under the Chronically Sick and Disabled Persons Act and will pay for personal care. Most departments, however, will be on the lookout for alternative sources of funding, whether it be a voluntary organization like the Spastics Society or even, in one case, the University Rugby Club, who paid for the care of a student injured while playing rugby.

Additional help

Community Service Volunteers also play a very important role in caring for some of our more severely disabled students. Most social services departments will see the benefit of paying for volunteers to care for a student rather than have him in costly residential care. The problem really comes when the student is already in residential care, when a case needs to be made for additional help to enable the student to study at college. But, even here, CSV have always managed to find financial help, even if it means applying to the Charitable Trusts or now the Snowdon Award scheme. When making out an application for a place at college, a student requiring CSV help will normally be expected to work out arrangements with CSV in advance, and submit them as part of the application. One result is, however, that it is not then possible to say whether an application has been turned down on the grounds of the student requiring personal care, or purely on academic grounds. What it is posssible to say is that, when it comes to requiring personal care, a great deal depends on how tenacious the student is, and how far and wide he is willing to look for help and for funding.

Open University students, of course, do not face this particular problem, except at summer school, but instead face all the difficulties associated with having to seek grants which fall within the discretionary powers of local education authorities. Like other disabled students, the Open University student faces the double problem of budgeting for the basic course requirements, while also meeting the additional costs imposed by disability. Local authorities, as we have now come to expect, differ widely in the extent to which they are willing to meet requests for help, but fortunately we have the very positive commitment of the Open University in its policy, 'that no student should be prevented from studying by lack of financial support'. The result of this policy is that in 1978 1.5 per cent of the total Open University population was made up of disabled students, but they produced 5.5 per cent of the requests to the Financial Assistance Fund for help.

Access and adaptation

There is finally a rather separate question to consider, namely the provision made by higher education colleges themselves. The Chronically Sick and Disabled Persons Act includes a reference to the need for access to university and college buildings but, without extra resources, with apparent lukewarm support from the University Grants Committee and with no special budget within the capital building programme, we have not seen the dramatic improvement in facilities that we would have hoped for. Whether the Private Members Bill sponsored by Dafydd Wigley brings improvement we shall have to wait and see. I somehow, however, have my doubts, for it is still not uncommon to see newly completed educational buildings that are inaccessible to the wheelchair bound person and display a gross lack of awareness on behalf of the designers.

In a time when the universities and polytechnics are facing serious cutbacks in their expenditure programme, it is surely not going to be any easier to argue the case for expenditure to facilitate disabled students. Already there are some who complain of having made expensive adaptations in the cause of one or two disabled students, only to have the facilities lay idle once they graduate, and we heard something about that this morning.

But to those who complain in this way, I would ask three questions. Firstly, what attempt have you made to publicize your facilities and recruit future generations of disabled students? Second, have you no disabled employees— not just disabled lecturers but administrative staff? I would guess that few universities and polytechnics and even student unions in this country employ their 3 per cent quota of disabled people. Third, if you believe as many people do, that educational buildings should be used more for community purposes, are not disabled people part of the community? We should also remember that building modification does not necessarily have to be seen as a major project. If I may quote Dr Gunn a second time, 'The prospect of a disabled student and his or her special needs does not have to be daunting—it may require imagination, ingenuity and flexibility of approach, but not necessarily large sums of money to radically alter every building'.

None the less there are occasions when relatively large sums of money do have to be spent. In such cases, the acceptance of a physically handicapped student should not have to wait upon the college making a windfall profit on its investments, or receiving a large bequest, as has happened in two recent cases. It is open to question as to how much an institution concerned with improvement of facilities for disabled students should have to bear the additional costs that special provision, equipment and aids demand. But what is clear is that there should be a systematic policy on behalf of central and local government and individual educational institutions, of accepting disabled students into further and higher education, together with a consciously planned and properly financed programme for bringing this about.

Attitudes to the disabled student

In this, as in other areas of provision I have mentioned, I believe there are one or two common threads which run through. First, in considering provision for the disabled student, the emphasis is still too often today on the problems rather than the needs of the disabled person. The difference really comes down to one of attitude. Instead of posing the question of, for example, 'what does a hearing-impaired student need?' or 'what might a student in a wheelchair need?', with the object of trying to meet those needs, the question is too often posed in terms of the disabled student being a problem; in which case the college has to decide whether or not it is going to take on the problem.

Allied to this is, I think, a general lack of positive commitment towards disabled students. How often when you look behind early examples of good practice do you find that they result from the great commitment of one or two individuals to the idea of integration. These have produced a snowball effect, and there are many more examples of good practice around, but it is perhaps in the area of financial provision that the overall lack of commitment is still the most obvious. As I have tried to illustrate in a number of instances, the financial provision is complex, the administration cumbersome and very wasteful, and the amount of effort required to be put in by the disabled student and his advisers is often inordinate. But in my view the complexity of provision should be seen as the symptom of the real problem, which is the general paucity of financial provision available for the disabled student.

Because there is no national policy for the financing of disabled students, we have the involvement of so many different agencies. It is the lack of financial provision that results in the complexity not the other way around. Those who mistake the complexity of financial provision as the cause and not the symptom of the problem, can, in my view, do considerable harm, particularly when the mistake leads them to call for a simplification of the system of provision. We have seen in other areas—and I am thinking particularly perhaps of the supplementary benefits system—that the simplification of a complex provision cannot of itself produce any improvement and can indeed result in great harm unless the individual needs of disabled people are taken into account. With a commitment to meet those needs, I believe we can overcome the barriers and provide equality of educational opportunity for handicapped students.

References

(1) J. SIMKINS and V. TICKNER (1978) *Whose Benefit?*, The Economist Intelligence Unit Ltd, London.

(2) A. HARRIS *et al.* (1974) *Handicapped and Impaired in Great Britain*, HMSO, London.

(3) NATIONAL INNOVATIONS CENTRE (1974) *Disabled Students in Higher Education*, London.

(4) CHARLES LULLYSTONE (1981) *Survey of Discretionary Awards system as it affects the further education of Handicapped Young People* (unpublished),Wiltshire Careers Service, Trowbridge.

(5) See, for example, M. HYMAN (1977) *The Extra Costs of Disabled Living*, National Fund for Research into Crippling Diseases; R. STOWELL (1980) *Disabled People on Supplementary Benefit* (SSRC Publication),Disablement Income Group, London.

DISCUSSION

Mr B. Massie, Royal Association for Disability and Rehabilitation, reiterated Mr Stowell's point on the complexity of financial provision, especially at the further education stage, which made the financing of higher education seem relatively simple. Further education was likely to be needed because of the lack of A level orientation in the schools, yet it was regarded by many as an expensive luxury, for which only discretionary grants were available.

It was often extremely difficult for a handicapped student to know for what he might be eligible and from whom, before even considering the complexities of the relevant rules and regulations. Having obtained a grant there was the question of whether it would really cover the cost of study for a handicapped person, which was often higher than for other students. (Some handicapped students joined the Youth Opportunity Programme simply because this at least gave them a regular basic wage of £23 per week.)

Whether or not the student actually managed to cross these procedural hurdles might depend on how helpful the local college's officers happened to be. Mr Massie himself had been given considerable assistance in finding additional funds by one of his college's officers; but, in some cases, officers might even resent the disabled student, feeling he or she might upset others.

However, where there was even one really committed individual on the LEA, or in a college or university the picture could be quite different; when he himself was a student, he had benefited from such an individual, who, when a new allowance was introduced, rang and told him what it was, and how to set about claiming it.

Normally students travelled well-charted routes through education, aided by a recognized 'highway code'; there was an entirely different 'highway code' for disabled students, and it had neither been published, nor considered by many of the educational institutions.

Mr D. Child, Association of Blind and Partially Sighted Teachers and Students, considered that finance, although posing acute problems, was only a practical matter - the additional cost of enabling several thousand disabled students to have parity with others in higher education was a very small sum in the total budget. The crucial point was commitment, or lack of it. Employers often claimed they admired the efforts of the disabled to overcome their handicaps and problems, but had insufficient commitment to carry through their ideas and offer a job. He said that he had been speaking to an employer on the telephone the previous day who said, 'I think you blind people are wonderful in what you achieve — I'm not sure how you manage it, but I know you do'. However, when Mr Child mentioned he was seeking employment, the employer said that he feared his staff wouldn't be able to cope with a blind colleague.

42

Similarly, when contacting the principal of a college for support, he received the reply that though the college was interested in what the Association were doing, they didn't concern themselves with the blind, and therefore didn't feel they could identify the college with the aims of the Association.

A very important element − indeed, perhaps the most important − of the work of the National Bureau for Handicapped Students was the overview it could offer on the needs of disabled students. An effective educational programme aimed at explaining these needs and how they might be met, to the universities and colleges, was crucial. As Ronald Sturt had said, money wouldn't necessarily solve the problems of communication within a large institution, or across institutions − it was organized commitment that was needed.

Whether or not a disabled person succeeded in further, and then higher, education still depended greatly on the tenacity of the individual; if the complexities of further education could be clarified − and here the Bureau had a vital role − then disabled students would more easily be able to take the first step towards higher education and, subsequently, employment.

The Chairman thanked the three speakers, and called for contributions from the floor.

A speaker asked if there was not the need for legislation against principals who, by refusing admission, discriminated against the disabled, although there would have to be exceptions where LEA's would not provide the necessary funds.

Mr J.A. Springett, Association of Metropolitan Authorities, said that LEAs did not exercise this sort of control; principals had to work within overall constraints, but the discretion was theirs.

Dr Margaret Agerholm, ILEA, felt that not only did the separate little 'pockets' of finance make an over-complex system, it was also an inadequate one. She felt most strongly that it was time to move away from a mobility allowance that left people immobile, an attendance allowance that did not cover the cost of attendance, and education allowances that clearly didn't cover the costs of education. What was needed − once the decision had been taken that someone was to have the educational opportunity − was for a body, possibly the Bureau, to add up the costs realistically and for them to be met from a single source. A collection of small sums of money which a student had to discover and which, when claimed and pooled, might or might not add up to the costs of education, was surely not an acceptable funding strategy.

Mr Massie agreed with this view, provided that in simplifying the system, the government did not in fact succeed in reducing it further.

Dr G. Grant, Medical Officer, Newcastle University, stressed that an attempt should be made to remove the many anomalies in the system of disabled student finance — for example, a partially sighted law student could not receive a grant for the purchase of equipment, as his course was not specifically 'training for employment'.

Dr Vivien Morris, Cranfield Institute of Technology, mentioned work being undertaken in the Institute's Fluid Engineering Department and funded by the Nuffield Foundation which might be of relevance, and asked that anyone interested, especially disabled graduates, contact her.

Dr A.L. Tait, University of East Anglia, pointed out that there was a need for someone, possibly the Bureau, to produce a really comprehensive national handbook, to act as a guide to the basic facilities, course availability, etc. as they applied to disabled students.

Mr Stowell noted, however, that such a handbook would perhaps be too general — there were many different degrees of disability; only by visiting a location could a student judge how such facilities (or lack of facilities) would affect himself or herself.

Mr Massie commented that, to avoid unnecessary and excessive time and travel, a general guide could be useful, if only to indicate which institutions were clearly inappropriate. However, the danger of such guides was that the importance of *facilities* could be exaggerated, to the detriment of considering whether, for example, the particular course content was what the student wished to study. Until an institution received an application, there was very little incentive to improve the facilities. Rather than a comprehensive guide, he felt there was a need for fact sheets, covering each university, which were available from a central source.

Mr Child reported that his Association had in recent years adopted a regional structure, with the result that their offices were valuable sources of local information.

Dr Roy Webberley, Senior Counsellor, Open University S.E. Region, pointed out that the disabled student currently seeking financial aid tended to be treated rather like an able-bodied applicant, whereas their specific needs should be accounted for. Hence it would be desirable to allocate some of the resources for disabled students as a block grant to universities and other institutions, so that they could allocate such funds to particular faculties, departments and so on.

Mr Ronald Sturt, National Bureau for Handicapped Students, commenting on the discussion made the point that, although practical problems of access were clearly important, they did tend to overshadow the important problem of how o *teach* the disabled. He wondered whether the Conference had concentrated on helping the disabled to reach higher education courses of study, at the expense of considering teaching techniques for the disabled. He emphasized that many forms of handicap simply made living and physical access difficult for the student, but that some, such as blindness and dyslexia, could pose grave teaching problems. The Conference had indeed concentrated too much on the first set of problems.

Miss Jean Birrell wound up the Session by stating that it had been wide ranging in its content rather than concentrating purely on the question of financial aid, which the three speakers had covered in some detail.

Idealism and realism

RHODES BOYSON

(Parliamentary Under Secretary of State with Responsibility for Higher Education)

The title of my talk is 'Idealism and Realism'. I do not mean this in a philosophical sense, with Platonism on one side and British Empiricism on the other. I would use the words more in the sense understood by G.K. Chesterton's 'Man on the Clapham Omnibus'. Idealism means what everybody wishes could be done, realism means what can be done in the particular circumstances and with the resources available. This does not mean to say that organizations, many of which are represented here today, will not and should not campaign but, at any given time, there is a certain amount of resources available, and the realism of the man on the Clapham omnibus comes in when he says, in the light of that amount, where the priorities should be.

We set out our policy on higher education for the handicapped or disabled student to some extent in the White Paper 'Special Needs in Education' which was published in August 1980. This states that some universities, polytechnics and other higher education establishments 'have developed and published arrangements for students with special needs on lines recommended by the Warnock Committee; and this may mean concentrating or rationalizing facilities in order to cope adequately with severely disabled students'. The paragraph in question, which is on page 12 of the White Paper, ends 'The Government is confident that all institutions will consider how further progress can be achieved within existing resources, bearing in mind the variety of sites and buildings involved'.

Categories of disablement

I must say here, however, that we are not concerned only with a variety of sites and buildings. One of the basic problems in this area is the very wide range of human needs covered by such terms as handicapped or disabled. In the context of higher education, about the only factor such students will have in common will be a pretty fair level of mental ability. They will all have managed to obtain some entry qualifications—and this also implies among them a good standard of personal qualities and what is called 'motivation'. I am well aware of the risk of considering that the only handicaps or disablements are those that have difficulty of locomotion, the wheelchair cases.

But there is beyond this a very wide range of need. At one end of the scale, those who have comparatively minor difficulties and have learnt to live with them—probably such people need only a little help to enable them to merge into the general student population and participate fully in the life of the college or institution. But at the other end of the scale, there are a smaller number of the very severely handicapped, who need nursing attention and constant attendance, where there are specific problems of integration within the university or higher education sector. Among the physically handicapped there are those with heart conditions, epilepsy, or perhaps haemophilia—the kind of condition that is not immediately obvious to fellow students, but is a very serious one to those concerned. In addition, there will always be those with varying degrees of deficient sight or hearing.

There is also a further category, which again in a way is different, those who might be called the 'newly disabled', whose trouble is the result of illness or traumatic injury occurring in or after adolescence. Of course, we cannot expect young people to wrap themselves up in cotton wool. I am not entering the argument (which goes on in the House of Commons and elsewhere) about motor-cycle riders, climbers and others, and the degree of risk that should be taken. If you take the risk out of life, part of life dies with it; one has to balance the two sides. But, undoubtedly, from this type of activity, and even from normal accidents some people are injured just before the time they come on to higher education, particularly by spinal injuries that condemn them to wheelchair life. These may need a special college such as Hereward, at Coventry—to get them used to their changed circumstances and to help them to catch up in their studies. But, at least they have their previous exper- . ience of normal (more common is perhaps a better way of putting it) life to draw on.

Exact figures are not available, but it can be said that the disabled form only a small percentage of the total student population. In higher education, there must be a similar spread to that in the whole population, from two or three per cent with very special disablement, which need special care all the time, to something like twenty per cent who have some special educational needs for at least some time. If we take the figure of twenty per cent, most of them can live an independent life as long as the authorities can make a few sensible arrangements and there is some goodwill and a little help from their fellow students. The really tough problems arise with a very small number who are very severely handicapped and who need very extensive support services— skilled staff or, perhaps, special apparatus. And, of course, we need money to pay for these services.

Rationalization

I now turn to the question of rationalization. The White Paper does talk about 'concentrating or rationalizing facilities'. If anyone were to say 'no expense must be spared when it comes to helping such unfortunate people', all of us would agree that this was a praiseworthy sentiment. But the doing is not nearly as easy as the saying. Perhaps the money available could go further, if we concentrated help for a certain type of disability in one institution of higher education as against trying to give less adequate help over a wider area. That is why I made my title Idealism and Realism. There must be a time when those lines have to cross: what all of us would like if endless resources were available; and what can be made available at any one time. To bring these two aspects into reality and to determine the priorities is, I believe, the task of all people involved in any form of judgement or administration.

In the Education Bill now before Parliament there is a strong emphasis on integrating even severely handicapped children into ordinary schools whenever this is at all possible. I agree with that, although I know that it is not over-whelmingly backed by people who teach in special schools. But I do think, other things being equal, that it does help if the severely handicapped can be integrated as far as possible in normal schools; obviously the same applies in higher education. Thus it seems likely that in future rather more students in the group we are discussing will have received at least part of their education in ordinary classes in ordinary schools, or in what we call 'non-advanced further education'. They will thus be familiar with life in the general student body and will look for the same sort of facilities in colleges and universities.

Choice of course

I should now like to say a few words about the important question of which course of study to choose. The careers officer plays a vital role not only in saying what jobs are available but in saying what one should do on the way to get that job. It seems to me that in many secondary schools the failure of the careers officer is in not getting in early enough in the second and third year to influence the course options that have to be done in the fourth and fifth year. Because, unless he is involved when those blocks of options are made, it is quite possible they will actually preclude students from various jobs. It is important that the advice given to the disabled, whatever their handicap, is frank and straight as to what they are most likely to be able to do at least as effectively as, and in certain cases more effectively than, those that are not suffering from any handicap at all. For example, there are some specialities involving field studies or some kind of laboratory work which are ruled out because the disabled student might endanger not only himself but also others in this, and he might not be able to do it fully. Whereas there are other jobs with possibly a kindred interest, that he could do at least as well as the non-handicapped.

Second, the choice of the very unusual or the recherché subject may present obvious difficulties. For example, the disabled student who wants to take a course in Sanskrit or Chinese will not find it easy to discover a university or college that offers these subjects and can also provide whatever special facilities he or she may need. Whereas, if the student chooses a more mainstream subject, we should be getting toward the point where the required facilities will be available.

Third, even with the best will in the world, establishments vary in the extent to which they can lend themselves—even with expensive adaptation—to the needs of the severely handicapped. There will always be some rooms in some buildings that are reached only by flights of stairs and where it is virtually impossible to provide either lifts or ramps. And this factor must rule out particular disciplines at particular establishments as far as the disabled student with some particular handicap is concerned.

Career counselling

Let me say something briefly on career counselling. As I have already said, I think this means beginning pre-O-level, and the more it is done with common sense and a full understanding of what can be achieved the better. The visually handicapped must, of course, avoid the wide range of occupations that entail driving a car, and a deaf student must be steered away from the kind of work —personnel work, for example— that in many cases can involve a great deal of talking and listening, which may be a heavy strain to him. The student has to look facts in the face, take all the limitations into account, and then go all out for a positive decision. The Careers Service can often help. Every local education authority has at least one specialist careers officer.

But what about those who—even after the best efforts of themselves and others—are unable to find a job? If, sadly, the disabled student has to face the prospect of living without work—or even of living in an institution of some kind—there is a sense in which this makes education all the more important. The dignity and quality of his life must be enhanced by the study of some subject which interests him, and the experience of student life should increase his capacity for independence.

The National Bureau for Handicapped Students has built up an information service that can provide such students with names of higher education establishments which may be able to accept them for a particular course, or meet a particular need. The Bureau has been known to go to considerable trouble to help students in this way, and I should like to take the opportunity, publicly, to pay tribute to that body and all that it has done.

While we are on this topic of admission procedures and selection, it is worth looking at the basic advice given in the UCCA's handbook 'How to apply for admission to a university'. 'Some universities', the Handbook says, 'can make provision for disabled or handicapped students. If you have a major physical disability (for example, if you use a wheelchair) you are advised first to consult the universities to which you wish to apply to see whether they can offer you the special facilities that you need'.

Students with a disability that ought to be taken into account are asked to enter details on the application form (I understand there has recently been a review of this but it will probably be some time before it actually is changed). The standard polytechnic application form also asks candidates to indicate if they have a physical or sensory handicap that might affect their studies or that would require special facilities or treatment.

There is, of course, plenty of scope for individual discretion here. Should a lightly handicapped student declare his disability, or hope to 'get by'? Nevertheless, concealment could obviously be a bad mistake if the student, having embarked on a course, finds himself in considerable and possibly insuperable difficulties. But if the college or university makes it plain that the needs of handicapped students will be sympathetically considered, this will not often happen. But I would still suggest that it would be best to lay it on the line from the beginning so there can be no misunderstanding.

Obviously, the decision whether or not to admit rests ultimately with the academic authority, and it can often be an extremely tricky decision, with a great number of factors to be taken into account. Can money be found for the additional building work needed to provide certain facilities? Will readers be available for blind students? How can the personality and capacity for independent living of each applicant be accurately assessed? I remember that when I returned from the Royal Navy to Manchester University to read history and politics, even at that time we had a blind student among the fifteen on our course. We had a rota, way back in 1949-50, of the hours during which we read to that student.

Access and building adaptation

I have already touched on the question of access and building adaptation that must always arise for wheelchair cases or others who have great difficulty in getting around. There is a very vocal school of thought on the 'idealist' side, which holds that every room and every facility must be accessible to such students. Where new buildings are discussed, this should at least be borne in mind as a general aim or principle. But at any time there is always a gap between how much money people want to spend and how much is available and there always have to be priorities. In the present climate of financial stringency, there is very little new building in prospect—it is at most a matter of improving existing stock. The scope for adaptation will obviously vary from college to college and building to building.Then there is the terrain—is it hilly or flat, or is it a split site?

The National Union of Students publishes a list of residential accommodation reported by colleges as possibly suitable for students with locomotive difficulties; this accommodation varies from groundfloor bedrooms to specialized units. Libraries, lecture rooms and communal recreational buildings are hardly less important, and there have, in fact, been a number of studies of access to buildings of that kind, including a particularly interesting one made by a wheelchair-bound student at Sheffield Polytechnic. This was the subject of his degree thesis. I am a great believer in consumer-orientated societies, and I am sure that his thesis was one of the most effective ones on the facilities that were available. He went round all the buildings—not only the ones he normally used—and built up a 'consumer's eye view' of the difficulties and possibilities of the different buildings. It is not known—and it is virtually impossible to find out—how much money has been laid out over recent years on improving access or providing facilities for the disabled. Specific items of work such as ramping are not recorded separately in the building plans, and the facilities incorporated in large buildings erected during the last few years have usually been allowed for in the design, and built at not much extra cost. But it seems to be true that ramps and other minor adaptations are appearing in fair numbers, and that wheelchair students are quite often seen now on more campuses than was the case earlier. On the whole, 'green field' campuses are more likely to be suitable. Intractable problems can arise in city centres, where blocks sometimes front on pavements, and there is no room for an outside ramp or for parking.

It is always interesting when one comes to a campus built in recent times, to see how much was absorbed and how much better it is than ten years ago. In my experience, it takes a long time, certainly in schools, for an idea originating from conferences like this actually to pass into normal practice and to result in better buildings.

My Department has, however, published a booklet (Design Note 18) about access for the physically disabled. This concerns educational buildings as a whole—not just those devoted to further or higher education, but the principles—pitch of ramps, sanitary provision, parking spaces—are of general application. A study of this booklet can be recommended as a help to not 'overlooking the obvious'. I am a great believer in the theme of never overlooking the obvious; so many people these days become experts in the minutiae that the obvious thing, which the non-specialist would have seen, is missed. This booklet lists the obvious factors that should be looked at, and it also suggests possibilities that might otherwise be missed. Of course, there will still be occasions when the authorities, after a very long and careful study of all the options, will come to the conclusion that their premises are inherently unsuitable for some of the physically handicapped, even with extensive and costly adaptation. And, when that happens, provided there are adequate facilities elsewhere, it would seem to me that it is not hard-hearted discrimination but realism. One cannot provide an overlap of facilities at every institution in the country, particularly if one is providing them properly at other places. The important point is to make sure there is a spread in different types of institution in different areas of the country to ensure that the facilities are there, somewhere within reach, if people actually want them.

Safety

I have not yet mentioned safety, which is a serious problem for those with limited mobility, particularly if they are unable to move under their own steam, even in an emergency. Tower blocks must be a nightmare in such cases. I have some in my constituency and I am certainly well aware now of their menace; they always have lifts but in cases of fire the lifts are taken out of action.

Exclusion of the handicapped from premises, even on safety grounds, is seen

52

by some people as a form of discrimination. The view of my Department is that the safety of everybody—that is, of the students and the staff and the disabled—must be an overriding consideration. Also, the legal requirements relating to health and safety and those of the Fire Office, must be observed. Of course, the Department is not alone in this; an intensive exercise undertaken by Liverpool Polytechnic has identified areas to which wheelchair cases should be admitted only if accompanied, so that in an emergency they could be evacuated by being carried—wheelchair and all, if necessary.

As for the less severely disabled, I have already referred to their natural desire to 'merge into the scenery' and to lead as normal a life as possible, with a certain amount of willing help from their fellow students. While this is to be encouraged, it is very important that the authorities should not *take for granted* that any significant help of this kind will necessarily be forthcoming. Many other students' first concern must obviously be to pursue their own studies and it is not fair to presume that they will have the time actually to put in that extra time to look after disabled students. To place in a hostel block a student who needs help with the operations of daily living—such as getting up in the morning—on the assumption that other students will *always,* I emphasize the word, help him can impose a heavy burden and will sometimes cause bad feeling. It can sometimes seriously handicap, in more ways than physically, the individual concerned. The arrangement at Liverpool Polytechnic to which I have referred, was made only after putting the matter to the Student Union and there was agreement that help would be given and given voluntarily.

Some examples of special care

Before concluding, perhaps you would bear with me for a few minutes if I give some actual examples of arrangements for the special care of disabled students that have been made by various universities and colleges, and commend them to show that we in the Department do consider that this is most important. I hope I shan't be accused of complacency if I say that I am heartened to find out how often the reality does actually reflect the ideal, or something pretty close to it; and to find how much we have done in certain areas or certain universities over the past few years.

A large number of universities and polytechnics are setting up special committees for the handicapped, for example, Birmingham University, Hatfield, Lanchester, Plymouth and Leicester Polytechnics. Special access maps for the handicapped are also being produced. In some places there are special student counsellors for the disabled, who keep in touch with students and their tutors and do any necessary trouble shooting.

The very severely handicapped sometimes have to be segregated –though, as I have said, this is to be avoided if at all possible. There are special residential units specially equipped and serviced for such students. Clarkson House at Southampton University will be known to many of you, and there is a unit also at Sussex University. Durham University has a support service for the profoundly deaf. This was started by the College of St Hilda and St Bede and has been funded with a pump-priming grant from the DES for several years. It has proved very successful and has now 'taken off' and is being subsumed in the University.

The City Literary Institute in London provides a support service for deaf students, explaining their needs to the staff, or transcription services. Warwick University has established a braille transcribing service for blind students, to whom the Royal National Institute for the Blind also gives a great deal of practical help.

I should also like to mention Community Volunteers (this is what I should like to think is a growth area)–young people who give a few months, or perhaps a year, to helping a severely handicapped student with his daily living needs.

My final example is by no means the least interesting and heartening. I can very sincerely–not just as a matter of politeness on this occasion–say how impressed I am by the services for disabled students provided from Walton Hall and from the Open University. It is, of course, true that the Open University by its very nature is peculiarly well adapted to the needs and limitations of such people. Nevertheless, the scale and scope of the provision seems to me to surpass all expectations as indeed has the success of the OU over the first ten years of its existence. I not only wish–I most confidently hope and expect–that this success will continue. That the OU has sponsored this conference on the disabled student is to its further credit. I have great respect and admiration for what the Open University has done and, within that, respect and admiration for what it has done for handicapped students of all types; it has been a pioneering institution respected throughout the world and one also respected by all of us in this country now.

In conclusion, let me say this, I have talked about the needs of handicapped students and what can be done to meet them, within existing resources and the balancing of their needs against other demands within our society. But let us not forget that many disabled students have a tremendous contribution to make to society if they obtain the higher education that their ability deserves. I should like to stress this because I believe we do good for them and we have an obligation to them; we should be doing it all the more because the disabled student has as much to put back into society and, in many cases, more to put back into society than anybody else. We are doing this, not just for a minority group in society with its rights, obligations and responsibilities, we are doing it because, by providing those facilities and by developing them over the years and giving proper guidance, the disabled themselves can actually enhance their achievements and their opportunities. By doing so they can play a bigger part in society for the good of all of us—handicapped or not.

DISCUSSION

Mr G. Bradley, City of Manchester College of Higher Education, suggested that the poor provision of facilities for the disabled student was more a question of the lack of will and commitment on the part of the Ministry than of a lack of available resource.

The Minister responded by emphasizing the effect that could be made upon departmental thinking by enlightened public opinion and a vocal lobby. He spoke of how impressed he was by the commitment of those concerned for the disabled as well as the disabled themselves.

Dr Margaret Agerholm, ILEA, was concerned that recently constructed buildings for higher education had proved unsuitable for disabled students and often required subsequent, very costly, adaptation.

The Minister said he was anxious to receive any evidence of such cases and would welcome specific advice on the inadequacy of current regulations.

Dr Agerholm said she was also of the opinion that many who taught in ordinary schools were not convinced that disabled students should be fully integrated with the non-disabled.

Dr Richard Holmes, Open University, taking up the theme of access to educational buildings for the disabled, suggested to the Minister that important clauses in the draft Bill currently passing through Parliament (as a result of the recommendations of the Warnock Committee) might have been struck out: the Minister agreed to check on this point.

Professor Marsland, Chairman of the Session, concluding the debate, urged all those who had other points to make, to write to the Minister direct, with specific examples of concern wherever possible. He then thanked the Minister, and closed the session.

Concluding remarks   R.M. Holmes, Open University

Dr Holmes said he felt that the Conference had provided a constructive opportunity for representatives of a wide variety of institutions to come together to exchange their information and experience on the topic of the disabled student in higher education. It might also help to allay the misgivings of some of those tackling this issue for the first time. He hoped that other institutions, not represented at the meeting, would also derive benefit from the published account of the Conference proceedings, which it was intended to publish by the end of the summer.

As the day had progressed, it had been possible to discern some common threads in the discussions, in particular:

1 The importance within each institution, of a senior committee with oversight of this area, and the need for an increase in commitment to the disabled student by institutions throughout the country.

2 The academic problems of access to the higher education sphere for the disabled, which were largely occasioned by the inadequacy and low expectations of the 'feeder systems' (e.g. access to A level study). These led to institutional misgivings about the possible lowering of academic standards.

3 The issue of whether it was possible or desirable to concentrate facilities for the disabled students in fewer institutions, which was allied to the problem of limited resource. The Open University offered one opportunity of higher education for the disabled — but it could not provide the ideal environment for many young students.

4 Fellow students were a useful support resource for their disabled colleagues, particularly for advice in course choice; but it was not proper for institutions to instate disabled students as the local source of advice and expertise. They had a full-time job being students.

5 A lack of unanimity on the issue of whether vocationally orientated courses were more appropriate for disabled students than 'intellectual interest' ones; some felt that this was a quite unacceptable attitude to adopt in institutions of higher education.

6 Post-O-level provision for the disabled in schools and the further education sector currently presented a significant problem. Many felt that both educational and financial provision remained inadequate and there had been little recent improvement in the access to buildings.

Dr Holmes then thanked the participants for their attendance and contributions. The Conference ended with Professor Marsland extending his thanks to the participants, and to the Vice-Chancellor of the Open University and his staff for their hospitality, and for the voluntary effort put in by the staff at all levels.

List of participants

AGERHOLM, Dr Margaret   OU Advisory Council on the Disabled

APPLETON, Mrs M.C.   Principal Lecturer in Education, Chester College of Higher Education

APRAHAMIAN, Mr H.F.   Senior Editor, Science, Open University

ARMSTRONG, Dr A.   Open University in Wales

ARMSTRONG, Dr D.V.   Deputy Director, Department of Extra Mural Studies, University of London

BAILEY, Mrs L.   Lecturer, Continuing Education, Open University

BAINBRIDGE, Dr Jean M.   Senior Medical Officer, Department of Health and Social Security

BARRY, Ms Charlotte   Times Higher Education Supplement

BATES, Miss D.F.   Careers teacher, Brookfield House School, Essex

BATTEN, Mr C.R.   Deputy Registrar (Students), Open University

BEAUMONT, Mrs S.   Mobility International

BECK, Dr Anne   Medical Officer, University of Leicester

BELL, Dr Mary   Staff Tutor, East Anglian Region, Open University, OU Advisory Council on the Disabled

BENSON, Mr J.T.   Association of Directors of Social Services in England and Wales; OU Advisory Council on the Disabled

BIELINSKI, Mr E.   Senior Careers Officer (Special Services), Convention of Scottish Local Authorities

BIRRELL, Miss Jean   Deputy Regional Director, West Midlands Region, Chairman of Committee on Disabled Students, Open University; OU Advisory Council on the Disabled

BOSWELL, Dr D.   Senior Lecturer, Social Sciences, Open University

BOYD, Mr I.H.   Director of Student Welfare Services, Victoria, University of Wellington, New Zealand

BOYSON, Dr R.   Parliamentary Under Secretary of State with Responsibility for Higher Education

BRADLEY, Mr G.   Principal Lecturer in Special Education, City of Manchester College of Higher Education

BRANDON, Mr W.   Permanent Secretary, Open University Students Association

BRECHIN, Mrs S.A.   Lecturer, Continuing Education, Open University

BRETT, Dr Judith   University Health Physician, University of London

BROADMEAD, Mr D.C.   Assistant Director (Student Affairs), Coventry (Lanchester) Polytechnic

BRYAN, Mr P.   Student, University of Birmingham

BUCKTON, Mr G.   Head of Student Services Centre, Plymouth Polytechnic

BUTCHER, Mrs K.   Administrative Assistant, University of Liverpool

BUTTERWORTH, Mr W.   Senior Counsellor, London Region, Open University (Retired)

BOOTH, Mr A.J.   Lecturer, Educational Studies, Open University

BARBY, Mr R.   Royal School for the Deaf

BROWN, Mr P.   Hemel Hempstead Evening Post

CAIRNS, Mr B.   'Adult Education'

CAMERON, Professor K.   Chairman of Committee for Disabled Students, University of Nottingham

CANTRELL, Dr E.G.   Senior Lecturer in Rehabilitation, University of Southampton

CARVER, Professor Vida   Continuing Education, Open University; OU Advisory Council on the Disabled

CARTER, Mr K.   Honorary Secretary, 'Active'

CASHMAN, Mrs C.   Nursing Sister, Huddersfield Polytechnic

CHAN, Ms S.   Assistant Registrar, University of Essex

CHAPMAN, Miss Lynne   Personal Counsellor, Communal Studies, Brighton Polytechnic

CHENNELL, Mr P   University of St Andrews

CHILD, Mr D.   Chairman, Association of Blind and Partially Sighted Teachers and Students

CHURTON, Mr J.A.   Welfare Director, Liverpool Polytechnic

CLARKE, Professor A.D.B.   Head of Department of Psychology, University of Hull

CLINCH, Mr D.J.   University Secretary, Open University

COE, Mr D.   Assistant Director, Student Services, Middlesex Polytechnic

COHN, Mr H.H.   Association of Blind and Partially Sighted Teachers and Students; OU Advisory Council on the Disabled

COOPE, Mr J.N.   Careers Adviser, University of Cambridge

COOPER, Mrs Cassie   Senior Student Counsellor, Harrow College of Higher Education

CORDELL, Dr R.   Staff Tutor, East Midlands Region, Open University

COTTERILL, Miss J. Royal Association for Disability and Rehabilitation; OU Advisory Council on the Disabled

CROOK, Mr C.A. Assistant Director, Leicester Polytechnic

CROXEN, Dr Mary Staff Tutor, South Region, Open University; OU Advisory Council on the Disabled

CUTRESS, Dr N. Senior Counsellor, West Midlands Region, Committee on Disabled Students, Open University

DALE, Miss Sheila M. Sub-Librarian, Open University

DAVIES, Mr E.C. Lecturer in Education, University of Durham

DAYAN, Mrs G. Special Careers Officer for the Handicapped, Institute of Careers Officers

DOBSON, Mrs Stella Head of Student Services Unit, Polytechnic of the South Bank

DOWNING, Mr A.P. Head of School of Social Service Studies, Bedford College of Higher Education

DRAYTON, Mr M. National Association of Teachers in Further and Higher Education; OU Advisory Council on the Disabled

EARL, Miss M.Z. Assistant Principal, City of Liverpool College of Higher Education

EVANS, Mr C.R. Senior Lecturer, Department of Psychology, Roehampton Institute of Higher Education

EVANS, Mr J.C. Deputy Director, Leeds Polytechnic

FISH, Mr J.R. Department of Education and Science; OU Advisory Council on the Disabled

FORD, Mr N. Counsellor, Trent Polytechnic

GARDNER, Dr H.W. University Medical Officer, University of Stirling

GAUNTLETT, Mr D. Research Psychologist, Institute of Educational Technology, Open University

GILES, Mr B. Manpower Services Commission; OU Advisory Council on the Disabled

GRAHAM, Mr C. Assistant Secretary, Department of Education and Science

GRANT, Dr G. OU Advisory Council on the Disabled

GREENALL, Mr J.C. Director of Information Services, Open University

GRIFFITHS, Mr R.E. Student Counsellor, Chelmer Institute of Higher Education

GUNN, Dr A.D.G. OU Advisory Council on the Disabled

HALES, Dr G. Research Fellow, Institute of Educational Technology, Open University, OU Advisory Council on the Disabled

HANSON, Ms A.   Assistant Senior Counsellor, North West Region, Open University

HARRISON, Mrs N.   Association of Metropolitan Authorities

HASLAM, Dr D.   Deputy Principal, Hertfordshire College of Higher Education

HENSHAW, Mr G.W.   Student Counsellor, Manchester Polytechnic

HESHEL, Ms Thena   'In Touch' and 'Does he take sugar', BBC

HOLDER, Miss C.E.   Warden/Lecturer in Social Work, University of Keele

HOLIDAY, Dr P.G.   University of Aston in Birmingham

HOLMES, Dr R.M.   Pro-Vice-Chancellor (Student Affairs) , Open University; OU Advisory Council on the Disabled

HORLOCK, Dr J.H.   Vice-Chancellor, Open University

HUGHES, Mr M.   Principal Lecturer, Special Education, Hull College of Higher Education

HEGARTY, Dr S.   National Foundation for Educational Research; OU Advisory Council on the Disabled

HULL, Mrs Jean   Senior Lecturer, Bretton Hall College of Higher Education

HUNT, Dr G.   Senior Tutor, University of Warwick

HUNTER-JOHNSON, Mrs E.J.   Secretary, Committee on Restrictions against Disabled People, Department of Health and Social Security

HUTCHINSON, Mr D.   National Council for Special Education

HURLEY, Dr Sue   Continuing Education, Open University

JAMES, Miss Wendy   Executive Officer, Polytechnic of North London

JEFFERY, Miss D.M.   Assistant Director and Dean of Students, Derby Lonsdale College of Higher Education

JORDAN, Mr D.H.   Senior Assistant Registrar, Open University

JUEL-JENSEN. Dr B.E.   University Medical Officer, University of Oxford

JACKSON, Dr J.   University of Strathclyde

KEILTHY, Mr T.P.   Chief Examinations Officer, Open University

KEKEWICH, Ms Lucille   Staff Tutor, London Region, Open University; OU Advisory Council on the Disabled

KIRKBY, Mrs J.   Senior Lecturer in Education, Edge Hill College of Higher Education

LAMBART, Mrs Audrey M.   Staff Tutor, East Anglia Region, Open University

LEARMONTH, Mr G. Assistant Senior Counsellor, Scottish Region, Open University

LILLIE, Mr C.   OU Advisory Council on the Disabled

MACMILLAN, Professor R. Head of School of Automotive Studies, Cranfield Institute of Technology

MARRIOT, Miss S.R. Secretary of Community Services, University of Sussex

MARSHALL, Mr G. Principal, Beaumont College, Spastics Society

MARSHALL, Mr L. Principal, Royal National College for the Blind

MARSLAND, Professor E.A. Pro-Vice-Chancellor, Vice-Principal and Chairman of Committee on Disabled Members of the University, University of Birmingham

MARTIN, Miss C.J. Administrative Officer, Student Affairs, University of Lancaster

MARTLEW, Dr Margaret Lecturer in Psychology, University of Sheffield

MASON, Mr P.J. Department of Health and Social Security

MASSIE, Mr B. Executive Assistant to Director, Royal Association for Disability and Rehabilitation

MATHIAS, Mrs A. Press Officer, Open University

MCALLISTER, Mr A.G. Principal, Hereward College of Higher Education

MCGINTY, Mrs J.C. H.M. Inspector of Schools, Department of Education and Science

MCLEISH, Dr R.D. Senior Lecturer, Department of Mechanical Engineering, University of Manchester Institute of Science and Technology

MCNAY, Mrs Pam President , Open University Students Association

MELTON, Mrs Jenny Assistant Summer Schools Officer, Open University

MESTON, Professor M.C. Vice-Principal, University of Aberdeen

MORGAN, Ms I. Milton Keynes Express

MORGAN, Miss M. Information Officer, Committee of Vice-Chancellors and Principals

MORRIS, Dr Vivien Senior Research Assistant, Cranfield Institute of Technology

MURRAY, Mrs S. Senior Student Counsellor, Dorset Institute of Higher Education

PARKER, Mr E. Pro-Vice-Chancellor, University of Salford

PATON, Mr W. Director of Student Advisory Services, University of Strathclyde

PHELPS, Mr P. Assistant Principal (Student Affairs), West Glamorgan Institute of Higher Education

PHILLIPS, Mr P.J. British Association for Hard of Hearing

POINTON, Miss A. BBC (Open University), Committee on Disabled Students

POLLARD, Dr D.R. Director, Modular Degree and Diploma Scheme, City of London Polytechnic

POWER, Mrs E. Disabled Student Officer, Open University

PRICE, Mr P.W. Senior Assistant Secretary, Council and External Affairs, Open University

PUGH, Mr A.K. Staff Tutor, Yorkshire Region, Committee on Disabled Students, Open University

QUINN, Mr M. University College of Cardiff

RATIGAN, Dr B.J. Senior Student Counsellor, University of Loughborough

RAWSON, Miss P.M. Counsellor, Student Service Unit, Ealing College of Higher Education

REA, Mr N. Provost, Langwith College, University of York

REASON, Dr D.A. Adviser for Handicapped Students, University of Kent at Canterbury

REDFORD, Mr A.P. Senior Lecturer, South Glamorgan Institute of Higher Education

ROLFE, Mr J.H. Head of Student Services, Newcastle upon Tyne Polytechnic

ROMER-ORMISTON, Mrs R. Secretary to President for England, International Year of Disabled People

ROYCE, Mr D. College Liaison Officer for Handicapped Students, Buckinghamshire College of Higher Education

RUMMENS, Mrs P. Assistant Senior Counsellor, South West Region, Open University

SAUNDERS, Mrs Valerie Administrative Assistant, Welfare, Open University Students Association

SCHOFIELD, Dr Marion Warden and Lecturer, University of Southampton

SHABAN, Mr N. Graduate, University of Surrey

SIMPSON, Mr T.S. British Deaf Association

SIMPSON, Mr R. Community Radio, Milton Keynes

SINGLETON, Mr J. BBC

SMITH, Mr C.W. Chief Summer Schools Officer, Open University

SMITH, Mr J. Head of Student Services, Bristol Polytechnic

SMITH, Professor N.J.D. Open University Council (Chairman of OU Advisory Council on the Disabled)

SNOWDON, Lord President for England, International Year of Disabled People

SPENCER-THOMAS, Mr O. Anglia Television

SPIERS, Dr S.P. Medical Officer, University of Loughborough

SPRINGETT, Mr J.A. Association of Metropolitan Authorities

SPRUCE, Mr D.   Acting Assistant Director of Studies, Regional Tutorial Services, Open University

STANLEY, Mr J.E.   Open University Students Association

STEWART, Mr J.   Editor, Association of Disabled Professionals House Bulletin

STOWELL, Mr R.   Director, National Bureau for Handicapped Students

STURT, Mr R.   National Bureau for Handicapped Students; OU Advisory Council on the Disabled

SWANN, Mr W.S.   Lecturer, Educational Studies, Open University; OU Advisory Council on the Disabled

SWEETING, Mr M.   Student Counsellor, Teesside Polytechnic

TAIT, Dr A.L.   Deputy Dean of Students, University of East Anglia

TAIT, Mr A.   Senior Counsellor, East Anglia Region, Committee on Disabled Students, Open University

TAYLOR, Miss M.H.   Director of Social Services, London Borough of Redbridge

THOMPSON, Mr N.B.W.   Under-Secretary, Department of Education and Science

TOMLINSON, Mr R.   Adviser on the Education of Disabled Students, Open University; OU Advisory Council on the Disabled

TROTMAN, Miss P.A.   Accommodation and Welfare Officer, Heriot-Watt University

TUCKER, Mr R.C.   Open Forum, BBC Television

UZZELL, Dr D.L.   Lecturer, Department of Linguistics and International Studies, University of Surrey

VINCENT, Dr A.T.   Senior Counsellor, North West Region, Open University

VIOLET, Miss V.   Marks and Spencer Limited

WAKEFIELD, Miss G.M.   Assistant Secretary, Council Division, Open University

WARD, Miss B.P.H.   Director, Crewe and Alsager College of Higher Education

WATKINS, Mrs M.L.   Electrical and Electronics Engineering Division, City University

WEBBERLEY, Mr R.   Senior Counsellor, South East Region, Open University; OU Advisory Council on the Disabled

WEBSTER, Mr P.   Director, Association for Independent Disabled Self Sufficiency

WELLER, Mr M.   Chairman, College Welfare Committee, Bulmershe College of Higher Education

WHEELER, Mr G. Open Forum, BBC Radio

WHITE, Mr B.W.H. Pro-Vice-Chancellor for Residential and Communal Policy, University of Aston in Birminham

WHITTINGTON, Mrs D. Ulster Polytechnic

WILLIAMS, Dr C.J.F. University of Bristol

WILSON, Mr D.H. Administrative Services Secretary, Queens University of Belfast

WOLF, Mr E. Midlands Council for the Preparatory Training of the Disabled

WOLF, Mrs R. Midlands Council for the Preparatory Training of the Disabled

WOODHEAD, Ms A. Royal National Institute for the Blind; OU Advisory Council on the Disabled

WOODWARD, Mr J.I. Disablement Information and Advice Line